Back Roads Bicycling

in Bucks County, Pa.

D0596786

Cover photo by David Graham
www.davidgrahamphotography.com

Special thanks to Curt and Judy Iden

ISBN 0-9714616-4-3

FREEWHEELING PRESS
P.O. Box 540
Lahaska PA 18931

www.freewheelingpress.com
info@freewheelingpress.com

Back Roads Bicycling

in Bucks County, Pa.

By Catherine D. Kerr

REVISED AND EXPANDED EDITION

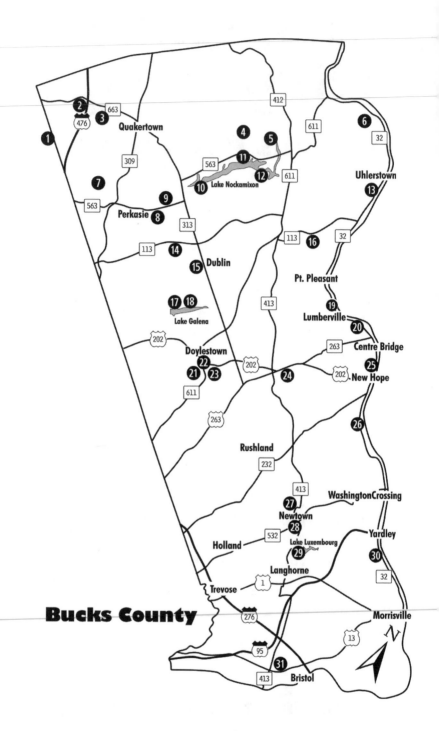

Bucks County

Contents

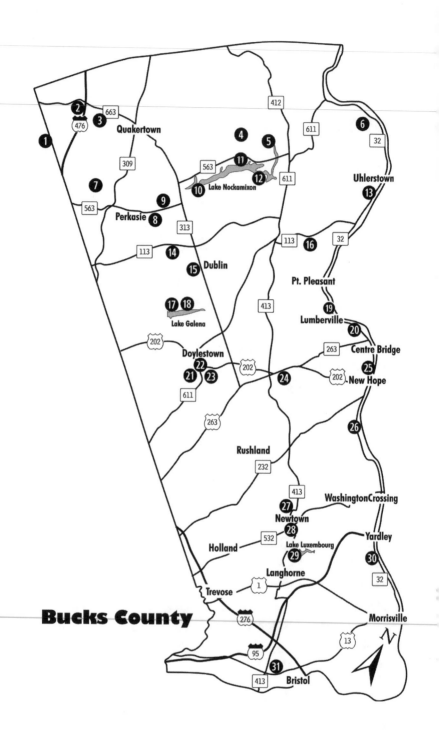

Bucks County

Quakertown

Lake Nockamixon

Uhlerstown

Perkasie

Dublin

Pt. Pleasant

Lake Galena

Lumberville

Centre Bridge

Doylestown

New Hope

Rushland

WashingtonCrossing

Newtown

Yardley

Lake Luxembourg

Holland

Langhorne

Trevose

Morrisville

Bristol

663
476
412
611
32
309
563
611
563
313
113
113
32
413
202
263
611
263
232
413
532
1
276
95
413
13
32

Using the cue sheets

The cue sheets in this book list cumulative mileage and use standard abbreviations to indicate turns:

R   Right

L   Left

S   Straight

X   Cross

BR   Bear right

BL   Bear left

Introduction

Bucks County is a great place for bicycling.

Rolling fields, stone farmhouses, red barns, Delaware River vistas, and quaint river towns head the list of scenic attractions making this a popular tourist destination.

There are routes for cyclists at every level. The long, flat towpath beside the Delaware provides extended opportunities for easy riding, while the hilly areas in the northern part of the county can be considerably more challenging. There's plenty of good riding in between, too.

If you live in Bucks County, consider yourself lucky. I hope the revised edition of *Back Roads Bicycling in Bucks County, Pa.* will help you find many new places to ride not far from home.

If you're just visiting, welcome. I hope you'll enjoy the routes in these pages enough to return.

This book is a completely revised and expanded version of the original volume, which was first published in 1998. A few routes were eliminated in areas where bridges have been closed or where changing traffic patterns have made roads unsafe or unpleasant for cycling. The book still avoids the heavily developed southern part of Bucks County, but it includes rides almost everywhere else, including quite a few that are brand new to this edition. In many cases you'll find long and short variations of the rides.

The rides are not rated. Ride difficulty is a subjective issue. Is a flat 25-mile route harder or easier than a hilly 12 miles? Instead of ratings, you'll find a brief description of each route, including information about how long it is and what kind of terrain it covers, so you can decide for yourself if it's the kind of ride you might enjoy.

Good maps and clear directions remain the heart of the book. The maps are designed to provide enough information to allow you to make short departures from the planned route or to find your way again if you happen to make a wrong turn, though they don't include every street.

The layout of the maps and cue sheets might seem odd, but the sideways design is intended to make the book easier to use. The perforations make it simple to remove pages if you don't wish to carry the entire volume along on your trip. The pages can be carried in a handlebar map case, and they will also fit into the kind of clear map case used by hikers.

All of the distances given are approximate. These numbers were calculated using a combination of car and bicycle odometers, GPS tracings, and mapping software. Unfortunately, each of these systems can be inaccurate. The figures are provided for guidance but they are estimates only.

Please observe the safety suggestions that follow. The routes described here were chosen carefully, but bicycling always involves a degree of risk. Riding on bike paths does not guarantee safety. Continuing development has led to increased car traffic all over Bucks County, and that trend shows no sign of abating. Choosing the right time of day to ride can make a big difference in how many cars will be sharing the road with you. Generally, early weekend mornings are the best times to ride, while the period from 3 to 6 P.M. weekdays probably is the worst.

Finally, I wish you all happy cycling—and I hope you have as much fun using this book as I've had putting it together.

Catherine D. Kerr

Safety guidelines

Every effort has been made to choose safe rides for this book. However, no matter how carefully a bicycle route is planned, it is impossible to eliminate all potential hazards or to foresee changes in road conditions. Even on bike paths and back roads, bicycling always involves a degree of risk.

Please ride carefully and use common sense. The League of American Bicyclists suggests the following guidelines for safe and enjoyable cycling:

Sharing the Path

1. Courtesy
- Respect other trail users; joggers, walkers, bladers, wheelchairs all have trail rights
- Respect slower cyclists; yield to slower users
- Obey speed limits; they are posted for your safety

2. Announce when passing
- Use a bell, horn or voice to indicate your intention to pass
- Warn others well in advance so you do not startle them
- Clearly announce "On your left" when passing

3. Yield when entering and crossing
- Yield to traffic at places where the trail crosses the road
- Yield to other users at trail intersections
- Slow down before intersections and when entering the trail from the road

4. Keep right
- Stay as close to the right as possible, except when passing
- Give yourself enough room to maneuver around any hazards
- Ride single file to avoid possible collisions with other trail users

5. Pass on left
- Scan ahead and behind before announcing your intention to pass another user
- Pull out only when you are sure the lane is clear
- Allow plenty of room, about two bike lengths, before moving back to the right

6. Be predictable
- Travel in a straight line unless you are avoiding hazards or passing
- Indicate your intention to turn or pass
- Warn other users of your intentions

7. Use lights at night
- Most trail users will not have lights at night; use a white front and red rear light
- Watch for walkers as you will overtake them the fastest
- Reflective clothing does not help in the absence of light

8. Do not block the trail
- For group rides, use no more than half the trail; don't hog the trail
- During heavy use periods (holidays and weekends) stay single file
- Stop and regroup completely off of the trail

9. Clean up litter
- Pack out more than you pack in
- Encourage others to respect the path
- Place all litter in its proper receptacle

10. Limitations for transportation
- Most paths were not designed for high-speed, high-volume traffic
- Use paths keeping in mind their recreational nature
- It might be faster to use roads and avoid the traffic on the paths during heavy use

Sharing the Road

1. Ride on the right
- Always ride in the same direction as traffic
- Use the lane furthest to the right that heads in the direction that you are traveling
- Slower moving cyclists and motorists stay to the right

2. On the road
- The same laws that apply to motorists apply to cyclists
- Obey all traffic control devices, such as stop signs, lights, and lane markings
- Always use hand signals to indicate your intention to stop or turn to motorists and cyclists

3. Always wear a properly fitting helmet
- Make sure that the helmet fits on top of the head, not tipped back
- Always wear a helmet while riding a bike, no matter how short the trip
- After a crash or any impact that affects your helmet, visible or not, replace it immediately

4. Ride predictably
- Ride in a straight line and don't swerve in the road or between parked cars
- Check for oncoming traffic before entering any street or intersection
- Anticipate hazards and adjust position in traffic accordingly

5. Be visible
- Wear brightly colored clothing at all times
- At night, use a white front light, red rear light or reflector and reflective tape or clothing
- Make eye contact with motorists to let them know you are there

© **2003, League of American Bicyclists**
Reprinted with permission

League of American Bicyclists
1612 K Street NW
Washington DC 20006-2082
202-822-1333
www.bikeleague.org

Bike paths

Delaware Canal paths

Distance: 60 miles, appoximately

Start: Access from Route 32 in Pennsylvania
or Route 29 in New Jersey

Terrain: Flat hard-packed gravel path

You don't have to be Lance Armstrong to have fun on two wheels. For those who take a more relaxed approach to cycling, the multi-use paths along the canals on either side of the Delaware River offer excellent opportunities to ride extended distances without encountering hills or drivers who don't seem inclined to share the road.

In Pennsylvania, the Delaware Canal runs from Bristol to Easton. It has been paved over in many places south of Morrisville, but from Morrisville north to Uhlerstown, the towpath is surfaced with hard-packed crushed stone, and the Pennsylvania Department of Conservation and Natural Resources is working to extend this bicycle-friendly surface all the way to Easton.

On the New Jersey side of the river, the former railroad right-of-way beside the Delaware & Raritan Canal has a similar hard-packed gravel surface. This path runs from Trenton to Frenchtown. Five Delaware River bridges in this area are accessible to bikes, creating opportunities for loop rides of varying lengths using the paths on both sides of the river.

The accompanying maps show places to park near the canals, and the chart gives distances between towns. Though a 70-mile circuit is possible, most cyclists will choose a shorter ride. There are several interesting possibilities. The loop through New Hope to Centre Bridge, Stockton, and back again through Lambertville is roughly 7 miles, for example, a distance that can be accomplished by casual riders in an hour or less. Of course, stopping to have lunch or do a little window-shopping can turn this into to a longer outing.

New Hope, the busiest of these towns, is popular with tourists who come to browse its many interesting shops and galleries. The Lock Tender's House Visitor Center on the canal at the south end of town has exhibits explaining the history of the canal, and a mule-drawn canal-boat ride is based there during the warmer months. Though the towpath appears to end just south of here, you can find it again by crossing South Main Street (Route 32), following the gravel road next to the canal all the way through Odette's restaurant parking lot, and crossing the small bridge over the canal just south of Odette's. The towpath narrows to pass a house and some condos before returning to a wooded, undeveloped landscape.

The canal paths on both sides of the river are multi-use trails, meaning you might encounter runners, bicyclists, equestrians (in Pennsylvania), and—in the winter months—cross-country skiers.

The shoulder along Route 29 between Lambertville and Frenchtown is wide and smooth, and some cyclists use it to make a loop ride with the canal path.

Distances between river crossings					
	Uhlerstown Frenchtown	Lumberville Bull's Island	Centre Bridge Stockton	New Hope Lambertville	Washington Crossing
Uhlerstown Frenchtown		9.4	12.6	16.1	22.8
Lumberville Bull's Island	9.4		3.2	6.7	13.4
Centre Bridge Stockton	12.6	3.2		3.5	10.2
New Hope Lambertville	16.1	6.7	3.5		6.7
Washington Crossing	22.8	13.4	1.2	6.7	

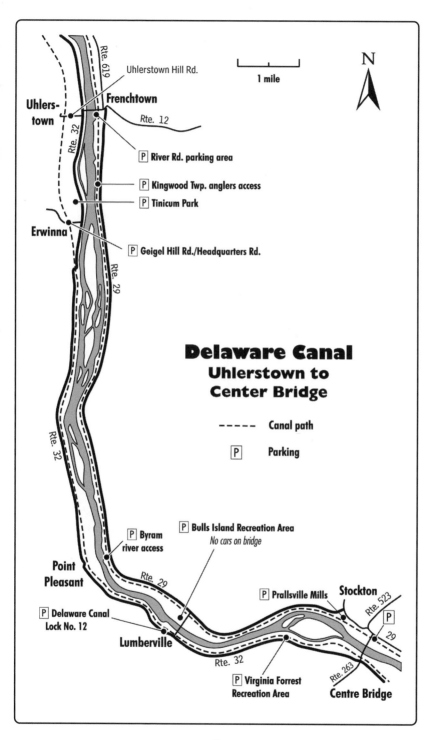

Uhlerstown Hill Rd.

1 mile

N

Rte. 619

Rte. 12

Uhlers-town

Frenchtown

Rte. 32

P River Rd. parking area

P Kingwood Twp. anglers access

P Tinicum Park

Erwinna

P Geigel Hill Rd./Headquarters Rd.

Rte. 29

Delaware Canal
Uhlerstown to
Center Bridge

- - - - - Canal path

P   Parking

Rte. 32

P Bulls Island Recreation Area
No cars on bridge

P Byram
river access

Point
Pleasant

Rte. 29

P Prallsville Mills   Stockton

Rte. 523

P

P Delaware Canal
Lock No. 12

Lumberville

Rte. 32

Rte. 29

Rte. 263

P Virginia Forrest
Recreation Area

Centre Bridge

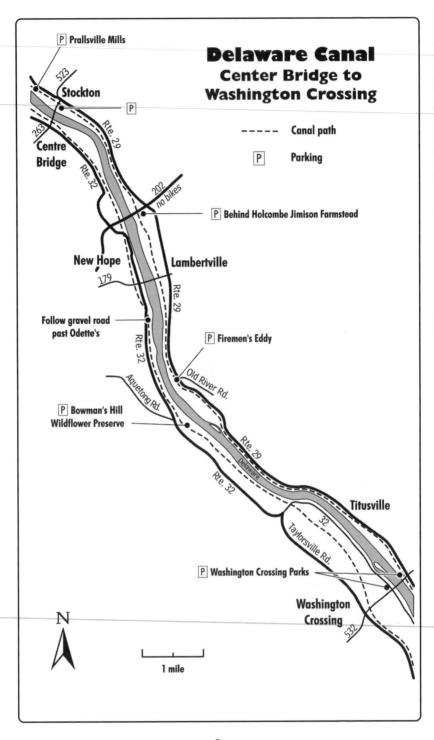

Delaware Canal
Center Bridge to Washington Crossing

P Prallsville Mills

523

Stockton

P

263

Centre
Bridge

Rte. 29

Rte. 32

202
no bikes

----- Canal path

P Parking

P Behind Holcombe Jimison Farmstead

New Hope

Lambertville

179

Rte. 29

Follow gravel road
past Odette's

Rte. 32

P Firemen's Eddy

Old River Rd.

Aquetong Rd.

P Bowman's Hill
Wildflower Preserve

Rte. 29

Delaware

Rte. 32

Titusville

32

Taylorsville Rd.

P Washington Crossing Parks

Washington
Crossing

532

N

1 mile

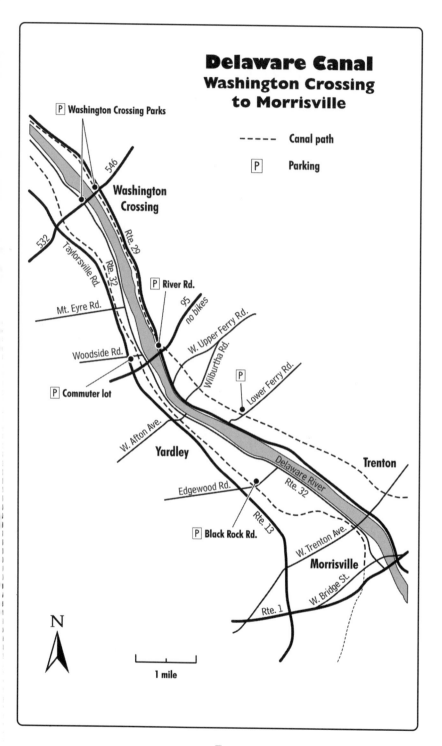

Delaware Canal
Washington Crossing
to Morrisville

- - - - - Canal path

P   Parking

P Washington Crossing Parks

546

Washington
Crossing

Rte. 29

532

Taylorsville Rd.

Rte. 32

P River Rd.

Mt. Eyre Rd.

95
no bikes

W. Upper Ferry Rd.

Wilburtha Rd.

P

Woodside Rd.

Lower Ferry Rd.

P Commuter lot

W. Afton Ave.

Yardley

Delaware River

Trenton

Rte. 32

Edgewood Rd.

Rte. 13

P Black Rock Rd.

W. Trenton Ave.

Morrisville

W. Bridge St.

Rte. 1

N

1 mile

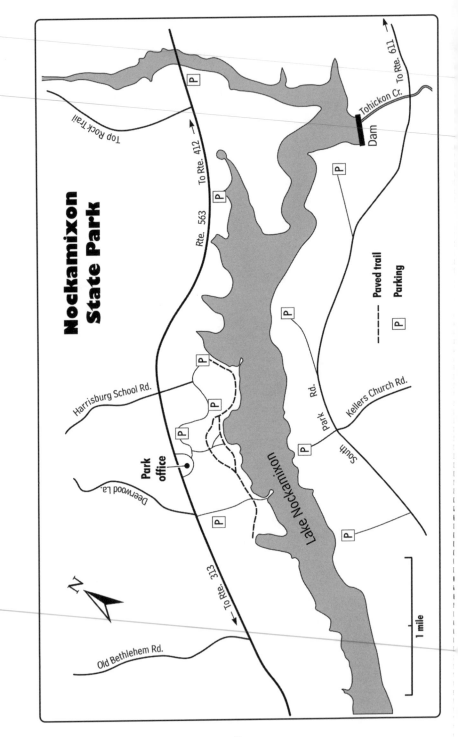

Nockamixon State Park

Top Rock Trail

Rte. 563

To Rte. 412

Harrisburg School Rd.

Deerwood La.

Park office

To Rte. 313

Old Bethlehem Rd.

Lake Nockamixon

South Park Rd.

Kellers Church Rd.

Tohickon Cr.

To Rte. 611

Dam

- - - Paved trail

P Parking

1 mile

N

Nockamixon State Park

Distance: 2.8 miles
Start: Nockamixon State Park
                Mountain View Drive, Haycock Township
Terrain: Rolling blacktop path

Nockamixon State Park surrounds beautiful Lake Nockamixon, one of the prettiest places anywhere in Bucks County. There are parking and picnic areas scattered all around the lake, which is 7 miles long. Park facilities emphasize boating but include a bicycle trail that is relatively short and easy, extending only 2.8 miles over rolling terrain that is suitable for all but the very youngest of bicycle riders.

Is it worth traveling all the way to this park to ride a 2.8-mile bike path? Quite possibly not, if cycling is the only thing you have in mind. If you're looking for a family outing including a variety of outdoor activities, however, the other park facilities can justify the journey.

Nockamixon has a boat-rental concession with canoes, motorboats, rowboats, sailboats, pedalboats, and pontoon boats. There are four boat-launch areas for those who bring their own. The park also has a fishing pier, equestrian trails (no bikes allowed), and a swimming pool.

The bike path begins at the marina by the main visitor center. It follows the edge of the lake past the boat-rental concession and ends at a cove beyond the fishing pier. (Another loop of the path goes to the swimming pool.) Watch out for cars when crossing the extension of Deerwood Lane near the fishing pier.

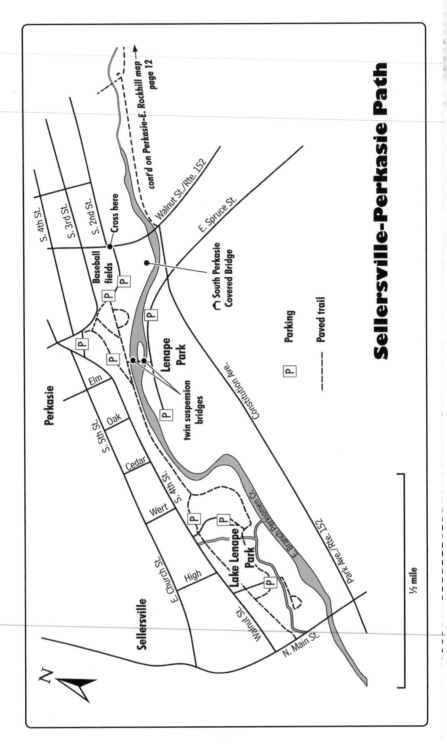

Sellersville-Perkasie Path

cont'd on Perkasie-E. Rockhill map → page 12

Parking

Paved trail

½ mile

N

Sellersville

Perkasie

S. 4th St.
S. 3rd St.
S. 2nd St.
Cross here

Baseball fields

South Perkasie Covered Bridge

Walnut St./Rte. 152

E. Spruce St.

Lenape Park

twin suspension bridges

Constitution Ave.

Elm
Oak
Cedar
Wert
High

S. 5th St.
S. 4th St.

E. Church St.

Lake Lenape Park

E. Branch Perkiomen Cr.

Walnut St.
N. Main St.

Park Ave./Rte. 152

10

Sellersville-Perkasie- East Rockhill Path

Distance: 3.3 miles
Start: Lake Lenape Park, Sellersville
            Lenape Park, Perkasie
            local roads along trail
Terrain: Flat blacktop path

In Sellersville, it's the Lenape Park Bike Path. In Perkasie, they call it the Perkasie Borough Bike Path. In East Rockhill Township, it becomes the Mervin C. Bryan Walking Path. And it's all part of the proposed Liberty Bell Trail, a multi-use path that would run from Norristown to Quakertown along the right-of-way of the old Liberty Bell trolley line.

Fortunately, despite the conflicting names, it isn't difficult to navigate this 3.3-mile paved path from Main Street in Sellersville to Schwenk Mill Road in East Rockhill Township. It changes character several times along the way, morphing from a park walkway to a trail through the woods to a path passing several new developments.

On its western end, the path begins in Sellersville's Lake Lenape Park and continues through Perkasie's Lenape Park. The two recreation areas sit side by side astride the East Branch of the Perkiomen Creek. Here it travels along the north side of the creek past grassy lawns and sports fields. It runs for about a mile through the parks, not including several side loops.

The parks are heavily used, and on this part of the path cyclists will almost certainly find themselves sharing the way with walkers of the human variety, and perhaps a few dogs as well. There are several points of interest here. In Lenape Park, the path passes a pair of small and rather unusual wooden suspension bridges, which were built in the 1930s by the federal Works

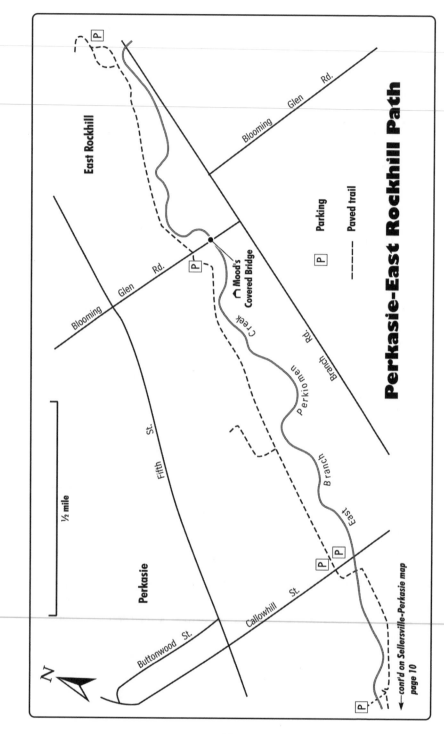

Perkasie-East Rockhill Path

East Rockhill

Perkasie

Blooming Glen Rd.

Blooming Glen Rd.

Fifth St.

Buttonwood St.

Callowhill St.

Mood's Covered Bridge

Perkiomen Creek

East Branch

Branch Rd.

½ mile

P Parking

----- Paved trail

cont'd on Sellersville-Perkasie map page 10

N

Progress Administration and connect the path to Lenape Island and a parking area off Constitution Avenue on the other side of the creek. Nearby, there's another interesting bridge, but this one doesn't go anywhere. The Old South Perkasie Covered Bridge, built in 1832, was moved to a field in the southeast corner of the park in the late 1950s.

The trail is continuous through the parks, but you have to cross Walnut Avenue and walk across the bridge over the Perkiomen Creek to continue from there. To get across Walnut, it's best to use the marked crossing with curb cuts near the driveway to the parking lot. Turn right on the sidewalk on the other side of Walnut and cross the bridge, and the path resumes on your left.

From Walnut Avenue east you're likely to encounter a lot less traffic, though cyclists do still have to share with others. This is a pleasant and rather scenic ride along the creek. On the way, you'll pass another covered bridge, Mood's Bridge, built in 1878, which carries Blooming Glen Road across the creek.

The Liberty Bell trolley was an electric streetcar that ran from Philadelphia to Allentown, ceasing operations in 1951. Some of the right-of-way no longer exists, but a feasibility study is in progress to consider whether it would be possible to use what's left to create a 25-mile trail through Bucks and Montgomery Counties, including this stretch through Sellersville, Perkasie, and East Rockhill Townships.

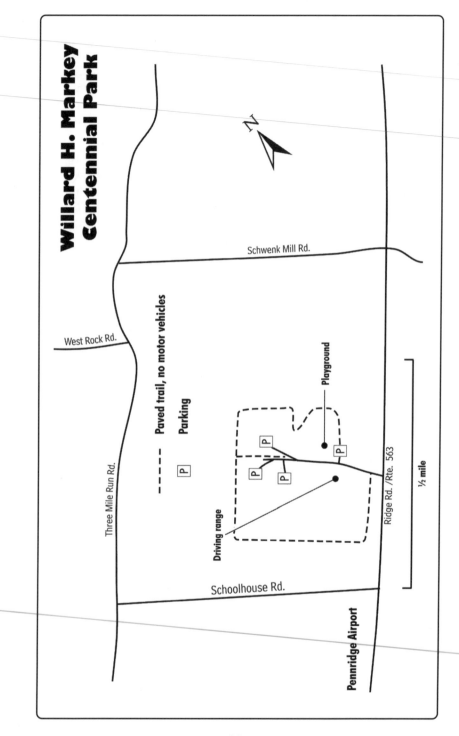

Willard H. Markey Centennial Park

N

Schwenk Mill Rd.

West Rock Rd.

Three Mile Run Rd.

- - - Paved trail, no motor vehicles

P Parking

Driving range

Playground

P
P
P
P
P

Ridge Rd. / Rte. 563

½ mile

Schoolhouse Rd.

Pennridge Airport

Willard H. Markey Centennial Park

Distance: 1.2 miles

Start: Willard H. Markey Centennial Park
Ridge Road, East Rockhill Township

Terrain: Flat blacktop path

The walking/biking path at Willard H. Markey Centennial Park in East Rockhill Township is pretty basic, but if you're looking for a short, level, safe place to roll, you might find that it's just what you had in mind.

The park is located on Route 563 (Ridge Road) between the East Rockhill municipal building and Pennridge Airport, just over a mile from the intersection of Routes 563 and 313. Its facilities include sports fields, a picnic pavilion, a volleyball court, a small playground, and a driving range that's open in the summer. The wide, level paved path extends 1.2 miles around the perimeter of the complex.

The path begins at the end of the parking lot next to the children's play area. Once you're on it, you really can't lose your way. An auto junkyard is visible through the trees close to the start; once you make the first turn, however, the view consists of cornfields and a distant tree-covered ridge in addition to the park facilities.

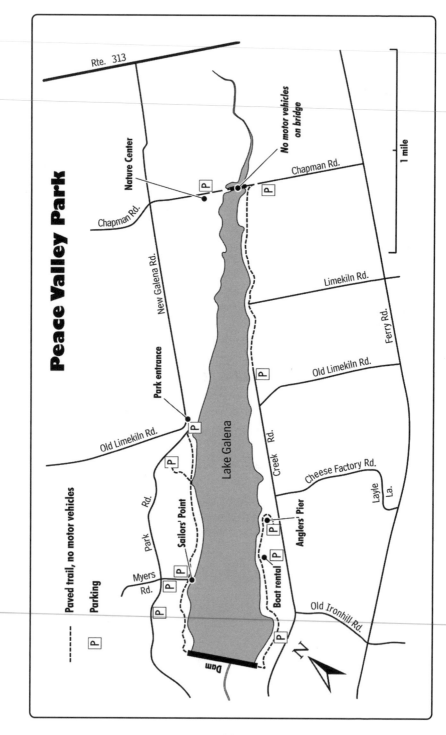

Peace Valley Park

Rte. 313

No motor vehicles on bridge

Nature Center

Chapman Rd.

Chapman Rd.

Park entrance

New Galena Rd.

Limekiln Rd.

Ferry Rd.

Old Limekiln Rd.

Old Limekiln Rd.

Lake Galena

Creek Rd.

Cheese Factory Rd.

Layle La.

Park Rd.

Sailors' Point

Anglers' Pier

Myers Rd.

Boat rental

Old Ironhill Rd.

Dam

N

1 mile

------ Paved trail, no motor vehicles

P Parking

Peace Valley Park

Distance: 6 miles, approximately
Start: Peace Valley Park
                New Britain Township
Terrain: Gently rolling blacktop path, local roads with
                minimal hills

The 6-mile circuit around Lake Galena in Peace Valley Park is quite simply one of the prettiest rides anywhere in Bucks County.

The path rolls gently past picnic areas and across the dam at the western end of the lake. There are no serious hills on this part of the route, and, for most of the way, you get great views of tree-covered hills across the water.

The county has been working on a plan to extend the paved path all the way around the lake, but until that happens, cyclists must travel nearly 3 miles on local roads to make the full circle. It's best to ride this loop in a clockwise direction. The only real climb you'll encounter going that way is on New Galena Road between the park entrance and Chapman Road, but it's a long, relatively gradual rise. Chapman is rather steeply downhill from New Galena to the Peace Valley Nature Center, however, and it's a tough hill to climb.

Peace Valley Park's facilities include boat rentals and fishing piers. The park also has 14 miles of unpaved nature trails, closed to bicycles, which are located mostly at the eastern end of the lake. A map showing these trails in detail is available at the Peace Valley Nature Center. To reach this area and the main park entrance, turn onto New Galena Road from Route 313.

Doylestown Bike & Hike

Delaware Valley College

New

Rte. 611

Rte. 202

Britain

Rd.

Lower State Rd.

Bittersweet Dr.

Radcliffe Dr.

Central Park

P   P

P

Doylestown Twp. Bldg.

Edison

Wells

Rd.

Turk Rd.

Windsor Way

Neshaminy Creek

N

- - - - - Paved trail

1 mile

Doylestown Bike & Hike

Distance: 2 miles
Start: Central Park
  Wells Road, Doylestown Township
Terrain: Rolling blacktop path

Most visitors to Central Park in Doylestown know the paved trail that circles the ampitheater near the Kids' Castle playground, but fewer find their way across Wells Road to follow the Doylestown Community Bike & Hike System down along the banks of Neshaminy Creek. That's a shame, because this loop offers more by way of scenery than most bike paths of its length.

Doylestown Borough and Doylestown Township have taken a leading role in Bucks County in planning for the needs of cyclists and pedestrians. (Lower Makefield Township also deserves mention for its efforts in this area.) The Doylestown system is designed to be utilitarian, but this section is also very pretty.

This ride starts at Wells Road near Central Park, which is located next to the Doylestown Township municipal complex. The paved path begins between a pair of wooden posts directly across from the park. Follow this path down to the creek and back up again into the development.

When the path ends, turn right onto Radcliffe Drive. You leave the asphalt bike/hike path at this point, but there isn't much traffic in the development. When you reach Wells Road again, turn right and follow the blacktop path back to Central Park.

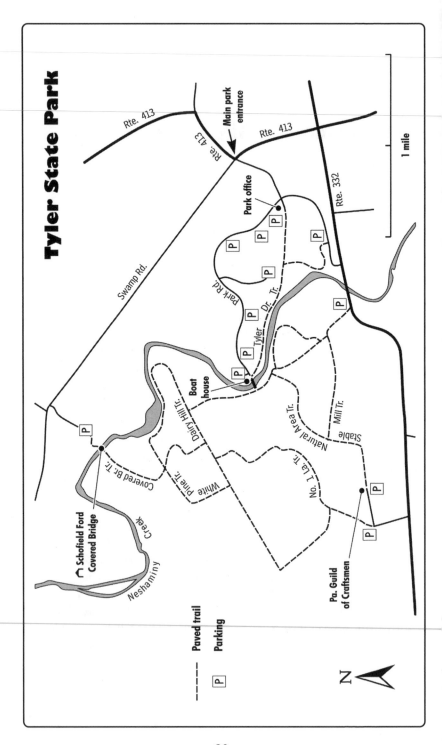

Tyler State Park

Legend:
- − − − Paved trail
- P Parking

Rte. 413

Main park entrance

Rte. 413

Rte. 413

Rte. 332

Swamp Rd.

Park office

Park Rd.

Tyler Dr. Tr.

Boat house

Dairy Hill Tr.

Covered Br. Tr.

White Pine Tr.

Natural Area Tr.

Mill Tr.

Stable

No. 1 a. Tr.

Schofield Ford Covered Bridge

Neshaminy Creek

Pa. Guild of Craftsmen

1 mile

N

20

Tyler State Park

Distance: 10.5 miles
Start: Tyler State Park
Swamp Road, Newtown Township
Terrain: Blacktop paths, hilly in some sections

Tyler State Park is known for its rolling hills, cultivated fields, old stone farmhouses, and the pedestrian causeway across the wide and scenic Neshaminy Creek. Tyler is especially popular with bicyclists because of the network of paved multi-use paths—10.5 miles of them—meandering through the park.

Because the park is quite hilly, especially on the west side of the creek, some of these trails are not good for novice cyclists. However, the Tyler Drive Trail is nearly flat for about three-quarters of a mile from the parking area near the causeway, and this section can be enjoyed even by small children.

You can get a copy of the official Tyler trail map at the park headquarters, located near the main entrance from Swamp Road, at the intersection with Route 413 near Newtown.

Check out the restored Schofield Ford Covered Bridge on the creek at the end of the Covered Bridge Trail. The original bridge at this site burned in 1991, but a group of volunteers built a replacement following the original design and using authentic materials and construction methods. The new bridge, which opened in 1997, can be reached via the Covered Bridge Trail from the main part of the park or by walking down an unpaved trail from a small parking area off Swamp Road.

The park is also known for its equestrian trails, which are unpaved. Though the word is that they are great for all-terrain bicycling, official park policy limits bicyclists to the paved paths.

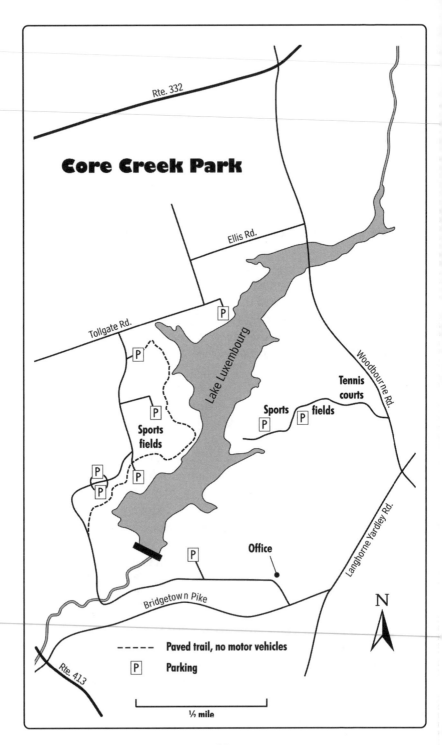

Core Creek Park

Rte. 332

Ellis Rd.

Tollgate Rd.

Lake Luxembourg

Woodbourne Rd.

Tennis courts

Sports fields

Sports fields

Langhorne Yardley Rd.

Office

Bridgetown Pike

Rte. 413

N

- - - - - Paved trail, no motor vehicles

P Parking

½ mile

Core Creek Park

Distance: 1 mile
Start: Core Creek Park
                East Bridgetown Pike, Middletown Township
Terrain: Rolling blacktop path

Core Creek Park is a wonderful place for a short, very easy bike ride along the path that skirts the shores of lovely Lake Luxembourg. The park bike path isn't much of a challenge, but it's a great place to bring a beginning rider for a taste of the fun longer bike rides can be.

As the map shows, the path begins at the parking lot near the northern park entrance and ends at the park road near the southern end of the lake. The path itself is a mile long. Bicyclists must share it with pedestrians and users of a variety of other wheeled conveyances including baby strollers, inline skates, and skateboards, so it's best to cycle here at times when the park isn't terribly busy—a summer weekday morning, for example. There is a small hill at the northern end of the path, but it is otherwise mostly gently rolling. For a longer ride, you can continue on the park road to the southern entrance; you'll encounter some automobile traffic, but it shouldn't be very heavy on a normal day.

Other popular activities at Core Creek Park, which is a Bucks County facility, include boating, picnicking, and romping at several playgrounds. The park is located just east of Route 413 in Middletown Township, and it can be reached from Tollgate Road on the north or Bridgetown Pike on the south.

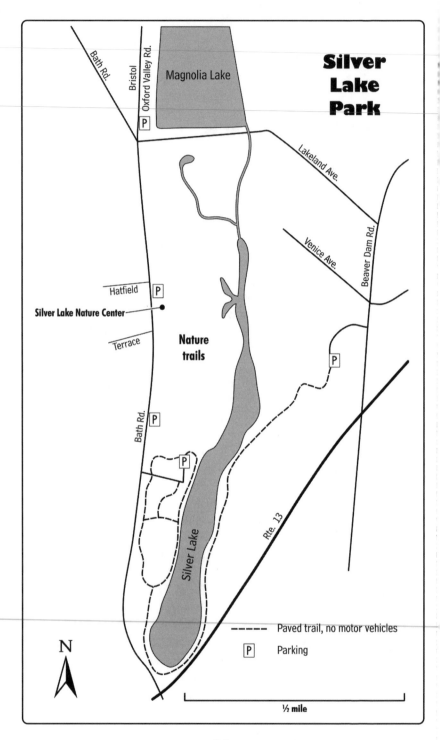

Silver Lake Park

Magnolia Lake

Bath Rd.

Bristol

Oxford Valley Rd.

P

Lakeland Ave.

Venice Ave.

Beaver Dam Rd.

Hatfield

P

Silver Lake Nature Center

Terrace

Nature trails

P

Bath Rd.

P

P

Rte. 13

Silver Lake

N

- - - - - Paved trail, no motor vehicles

P   Parking

½ mile

Silver Lake Park

Distance: 1.5 miles
Start: Silver Lake Park
         Bath Road, Bristol Township
Terrain: Flat blacktop path

Silver Lake Park's location between busy Route 13, Bath Road, and the Pennsylvania Turnpike will not strike most nature lovers as particularly promising, yet it does manage to have the feeling of a place set apart from its surroundings.

The lake attracts geese and other waterfowl, which in turn draw binocular-bearing bird-watchers to the 235 acres of the Silver Lake Nature Center. A 4.5-mile network of trails in this part of the park is intended for hikers rather than cyclists, but it's worth a visit if you have the time. You can get a detailed trail map at the nature center building, which also has interpretive exhibits and a gift shop.

The public recreation area to the south of the nature center has parking, a small playground, barbecue grills, and picnic tables. The paved multi-use path begins in this area and runs about a mile around the bottom of the lake to another parking lot on the other side.

Rides

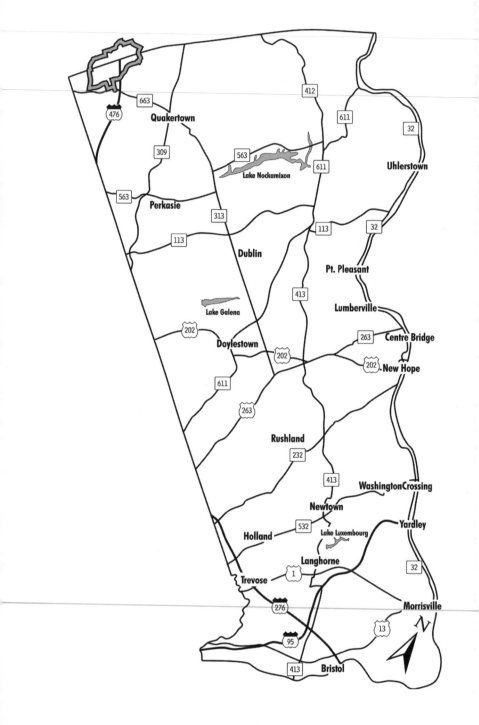

Spinnerstown

Distance: 12.0 miles

Start: Molasses Creek Park
Krammes Road, Milford Township

Terrain: Rolling country roads with some hills

This ride in the northwest corner of the county includes a mix of farmland and woods in an area that still has a rural feel despite increasing development spurred by its proximity to the Northeast Extension of the Pennsylvania Turnpike.

Many roads along this ride are poorly marked, which unfortunately is not uncommon in northern Bucks County. Don't hesitate to consult the route map from time to time to make sure you are where you want to be.

The most accessible parking for the ride is just south of Route 663 at Molasses Creek Park, across Krammes Road from the Milford Township Building. Although Route 663 is a busy road, a traffic light facilitates crossing to the north side. Be warned, however, that it is a short light.

The first stretch of Spinnerstown Road can be somewhat busy, but once you turn onto Steinsburg Road, there is less traffic. (The sign on the left at this turn says Sleepy Hollow Road, but the road to the right is Steinsburg.)

There's a steep uphill on East Mill Hill Road (near the orchard suggested by the name Orchard Road) just before you reach Landis Lane. If you stop to rest here, be sure to turn around and admire the scenic vista behind you.

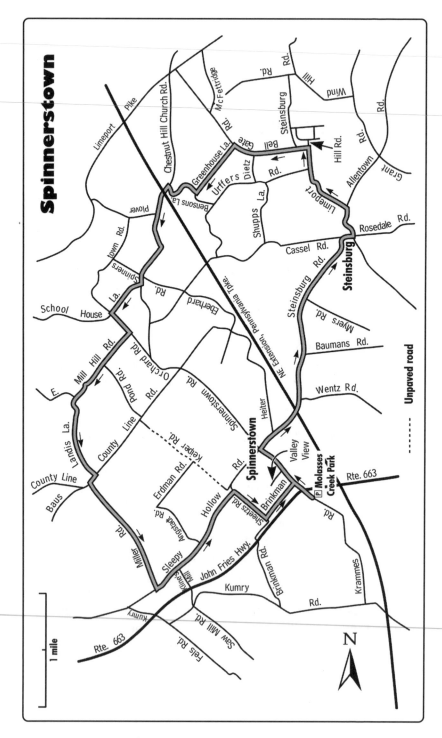

Spinnerstown

Unpaved road

N

1 mile

Spinnerstown

P		Molasses Creek Park, Krammes Rd., Milford Twp.
0.0	R	Krammes Rd.
0.1	X	Rte. 663/John Fries Hwy.
0.7	R	Steinsburg Rd.
2.8	R	Steinsburg Rd.
2.9	L	Allentown Rd.
3.2	L	Limeport Rd.
4.0	L	Bell Gate Rd.
4.6	L	Greenhouse La.
5.1	R	Benson La.
5.5	L	Chestnut Hill Church Rd.
6.4	X	Eberhard Rd.
6.5	R	School House La.
6.9	L	Orchard Rd.
7.1	R	E. Mill Hill Rd.
7.9	S	Landis La.
8.7	R	County Line Rd.
8.8	L	Miller Rd.
9.9	L	Sleepy Hollow Rd.
11.0	R	Sheetzs Rd.
11.4	L	Brinkman Rd.
11.8	R	Spinnerstown Rd.
11.9	X	Rte. 663/John Fries Hwy.
12.0	L	Return to Molasses Creek Park

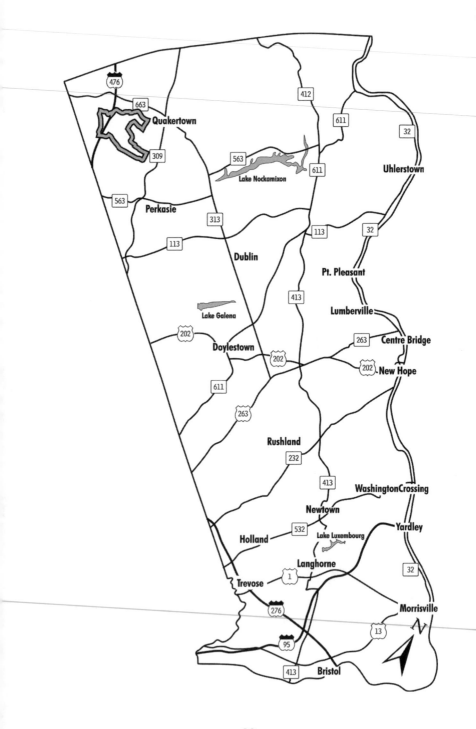

Trumbauersville

Distance: 13.4 miles
Start: Millford Township Park
Mill Road, Milford Township
Terrain: Rolling country roads with some hills; alternate
route includes one steep hill

Not far from Quakertown and busy Route 309, this route
passes through the town of Trumbauersville yet still feels like a
ride in the country.

It begins at the Milford Township Park located on Unami
Creek, off Allentown Road. For the first half mile or so the ride
goes along Mill Road, which is lightly traveled and nearly level as
it follows the bank of the creek.

On the other side of Creamery Road, Mill Road leaves the
woods and goes through farmland. Eventually, the route passes
several developments and goes through the town of Trumbauersville. After you leave town, Camp Rockhill Road and Esten Road
offer pleasant views to the south. Finally, the route enters the
woods and follows the creek back to the park.

For nearly a hundred years, Allentown Road crossed the Unami on a one-lane humpback bridge known as Campbell's Bridge.
Then the Pennsylvania Department of Transportation decided
to replace the bridge, which is located next to Milford Township
Park. This means that Allentown Road will be impassable here
for about a year once construction begins. An alternate route is
provided in case you find the bridge closed.

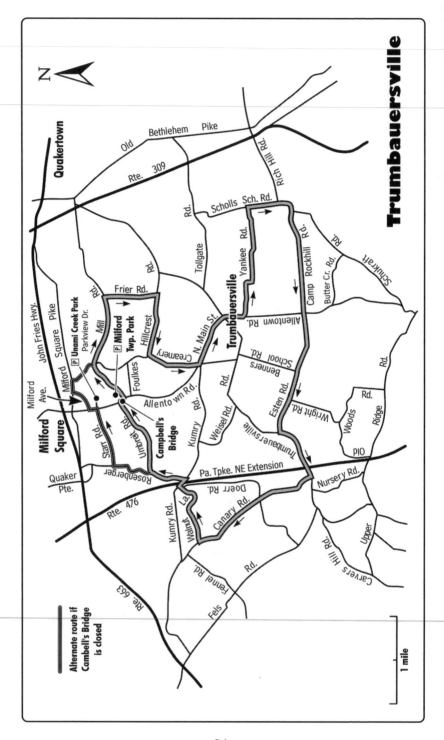

Trumbauersville

N

Quakertown

Old Bethlehem Pike

Rte. 309

Scholls Sch. Rd.

Rich Hill Rd.

Tollgate Rd.

Rd.

Yankee Rd.

Camp Rockhill Rd.

Butter Cr. Rd.

Schukraft Rd.

Frier Rd.

Mill Rd.

Parkview Dr.

P Unami Creek Park

P Milford Twp. Park

Hillcrest

Creamery

N. Main St.

Trumbauersville

Allentown Rd.

Benners School Rd.

Rd.

Milford Square Pike

John Fries Hwy.

Milford Ave.

Milford Square

Milford Sq.

Foulkes

Allentown Rd.

Kumry Rd.

Weisel Rd.

Esten Rd.

Wright Rd.

Woods Rd.

Ridge Rd.

Old

Starr Rd.

Umbrel Rd.

Campbell's Bridge

Roesenberger Rd.

Quaker Pte.

Rte. 476

Pa. Tpke. NE Extension

Trumbauersville Rd.

Doerr Rd.

Nursery Rd.

Walnut La.

Canary Rd.

Kumry Rd.

Fennel Rd.

Fels Rd.

Rte. 663

Carver's Hill Rd.

Upper

Alternate route if Cambell's Bridge is closed

1 mile

Trumbauersville

P		Milford Twp. Park, Mill Rd., Milford Twp.
0.0	L	Ride east on Mill Rd.
0.5	X	Creamery Rd.
1.3	R	Frier Rd.
2.0	R	Hillcrest Rd.
2.7	L	Creamery Rd.
3.3	L	N. Main St.
4.2	L	Yankee Rd.
5.6	R	Scholl's School Rd.
6.2	S	Camp Rockhill Rd.
7.4	X	Allentown Rd.
	S	Esten Rd.
8.8	L	Trumbauersville Rd.
9.4	X	Rte. 476
9.5	R	Canary Rd.
11.1	R	Walnut La.
11.9	R	Kumry Rd.
12.0	L	Rosenberger Rd.
12.4	R	Umbreit Rd.
13.3	R	Allentown Rd.
13.4	L	Mill Rd.
13.4	L	Return to Milford Twp. Park

Aternate route
if Campbell's Bridge is closed

P		Unami Creek Park Parkview Dr., Milford Twp.
0.0	L	Parkview Dr.
0.1	R	Allentown Rd.
0.2	R	Milford Ave.
0.5	R	Milford Square Pike
0.6	R	Hillcrest Rd.
1.0	L	Mill Rd.
1.8	R	Frier Rd.
2.5	R	Hillcrest Rd.
3.2	L	Creamery Rd.
3.8	L	N. Main St.
4.7	L	Yankee Rd.
6.1	R	Scholl's School Rd.
6.6	S	Camp Rockhill Rd.
7.9	X	Allentown Rd.
	S	Esten Rd.
9.3	L	Trumbauersville Rd.
9.9	X	Rte. 476
10.0	R	Canary Rd.
11.6	R	Walnut La.
12.4	R	Kumry Rd.
12.5	L	Rosenberger Rd.
13.4	R	Starr Rd.
14.1	X	Allentown Rd.
	S	Parkview Dr.
14.2	R	Return to Unami Creek Park

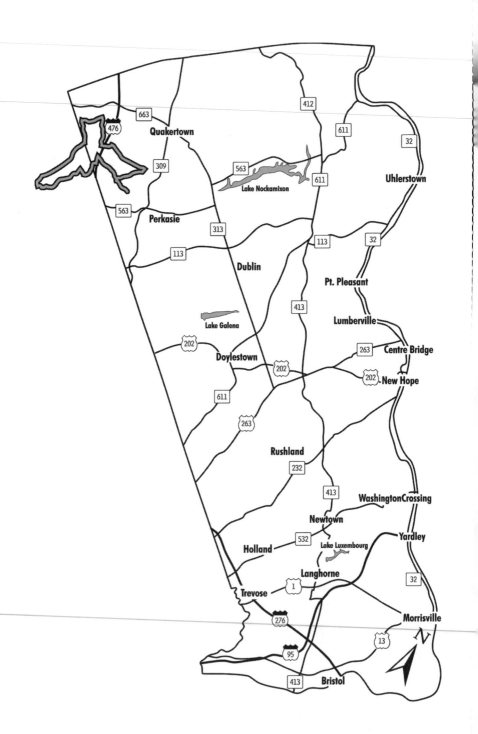

Unami Creek

Distance: 23.8 miles

Start: State Game Lands 196 parking area
Upper Ridge Road, Milford Township

Terrain: Hilly country roads with several steep climbs and descents; 0.8 miles unpaved

Variation: 16.4 miles on hilly country roads; 0.8 miles unpaved

This is a challenging ride with some wonderful scenery as payback.

The highlight of the route is a 3.4-mile stretch of Swamp Creek Road running beside Unami Creek in a valley so deep it might come as a surprise to find the sun still shining when you finally climb out of it. The creek is wide and dramatically strewn with huge boulders. This area is home to a large Boy Scout reservation, but otherwise sparsely populated.

Also noteworthy are Camp Rockhill and Esten Roads, with sweeping vistas to the south, and unpaved Long Road, which passes Camp Skymount, a Marlborough Township park set on a lake.

The ride begins in an unpaved parking area on the south side of Ridge Valley Road. The lot, part of the 423-acre State Game Lands 196, is located a short distance east of the main game lands parking area.

The route goes up and down several steep hills. Be especially careful on Allentown Road near the beginning of the ride, where the road is both steep and winding as it passes between deposits of boulders like those that dot Unami Creek. The route given as a variation avoids this hill (although it is far from flat) without sacrificing the most dramatic scenery on the ride.

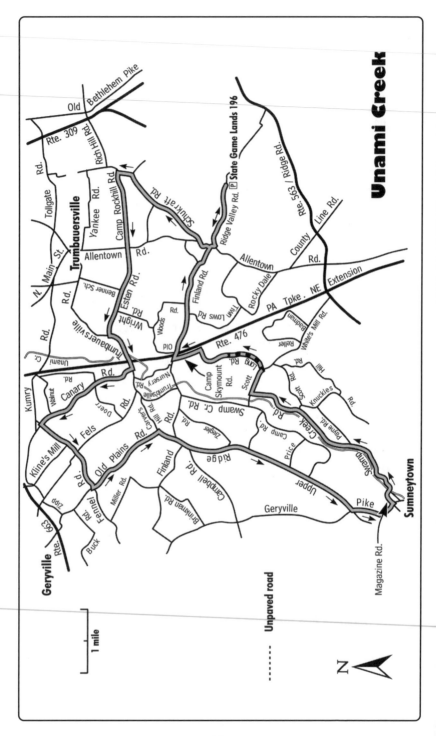

Unami Creek

🅿 State Game Lands 196

Trumbauersville

Geryville

Sumneytown

Old Bethlehem Pike
Rte. 309
Rich Hill Rd.
Tollgate Rd.
Rd.
N. Main St.
Yankee Rd.
Camp Rockhill Rd.
Allentown Rd.
Benner Sch.
Wright Esten Rd.
Schukraft Rd.
Ridge Valley Rd.
Rte. 563 / Ridge Rd.
Allentown
County Line Rd.
Rd.
Rocky Dale
Finland Rd.
Twin Lows Rd.
PA Tpke. NE Extension
Woods Rd.
PIO
Rte. 476
Radman
Reller
White's Mill Rd.
Trumbauersville Rd.
Unami Cr.
Kumry Rd.
Walnut
Canary Rd.
Doerr Rd.
Rd.
Nursery Rd.
Camp Skymount Rd.
Long Rd.
Scott Rd.
Swamp Cr. Rd.
Scott Rd.
Hill Rd.
Knuckles Rd.
Fels
Old Plains Rd.
Carvers Rd.
Hill Rd.
Ziegler Rd.
Camp Rd.
Price
Creek Rd.
Payne Rd.
Kline's Mill Rd.
Fennel Rd.
Zipp
Buck Rd.
Miller Rd.
Finland Rd.
Brinman Rd.
Campbell Rd.
Ridge
Upper Geryville
Swamp
Pike
Magazine Rd.
Rte. 663

1 mile

- - - - - Unpaved road

N

Unami Creek

P		Game Lands 196 parking area, Ridge Valley Rd., W. Rockhill Twp.
0.0	L	Ridge Valley Rd.
1.0	R	Allentown Rd.
1.2	R	Schukraft Rd.
3.1	L	Camp Rockhill Rd.
4.3	X	Allentown Rd.
	S	Continue on Esten Rd.
5.8	L	Trumbauersville Rd.
6.3	X	Pa. Tpke. NE Extension
6.4	R	Canary Rd.
8.3	L	Fennel Rd.
9.6	L	Old Plains Rd.
11.1	R	Carver's Hill Rd.
		BECOMES HARING RD.
11.4	R	Upper Ridge Rd.

14.6	L	Geryville Pike
15.3	L	Magazine Rd.
15.6	S	Swamp Creek Rd.
18.6	R	Scott Rd.
19.0	L	Long Rd.
		UNPAVED NEXT 0.8 MILES; BECOMES CAMP SKYMOUNT RD.
20.8	R	Upper Ridge Rd.
		BECOMES FINLAND RD.
22.7	R	Allentown Rd.
22.8	L	Upper Ridge Rd.
23.8	R	Return to state game lands parking area

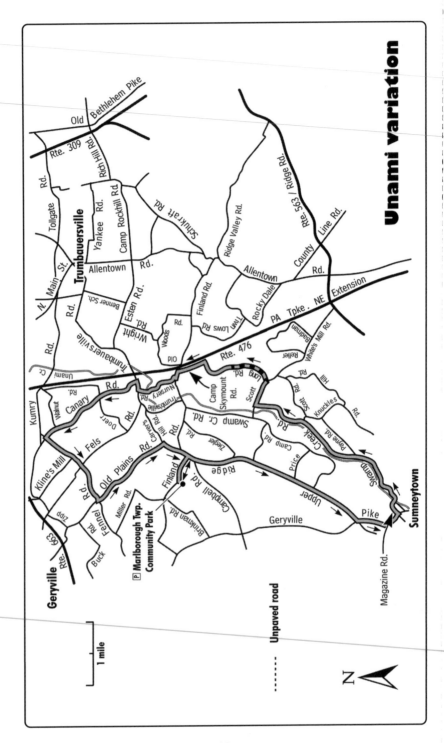

Unami Variation

Unami variation

P **Marlborough Twp. Community Park, Finland Rd., Marlborough Twp.**

0.0	R	Finland Rd.
0.4	R	Upper Ridge Rd.
3.5	L	Geryville Pike
4.4	L	Magazine Rd.
4.7	S	Swamp Creek Rd.
7.7	R	Scott Rd.
8.1	L	Long Rd.

UNPAVED NEXT 0.8 MILES;
BECOMES CAMP SKYMOUNT RD.

9.9	L	Upper Ridge Rd.
10.0	R	Nursery Rd.
10.7	R	Trumbauersville Rd.
10.9	L	Canary Rd.
12.7	L	Fennel Rd.
14.1	L	Old Plains Rd.

15.6	R	Carver's Hill Rd.

BECOMES HARING RD.

16.0	R	Finland Rd.
16.4	L	Return to Marlborough Township Community Park

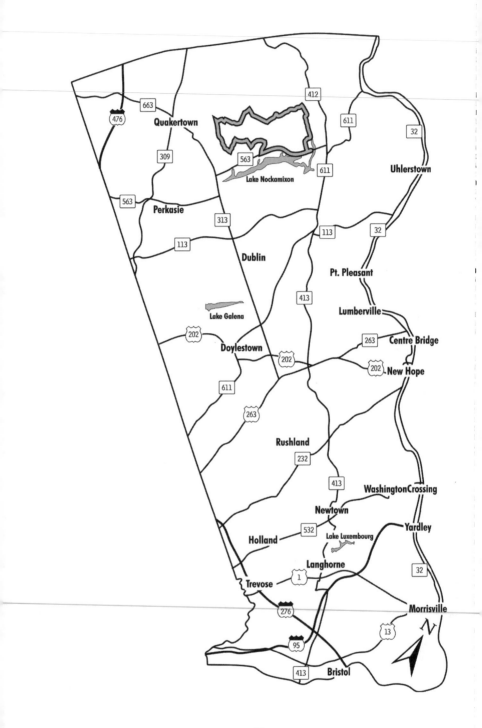

Haycock Mountain

Distance: 19.6 miles

Start: State Game Lands 157 parking area
Upper Ridge Road, Milford Township

Terrain: Rolling country roads; wide shoulder on Route 563

Variations: 10.2 and 13.5 miles on rolling country roads

Haycock Mountain tops out at about 970 feet, tall enough to be visible from much of northern Bucks County. Oddly, though this ride circles Haycock's base, you can't really see the mountain from anywhere on the route. The terrain here is rolling but includes no serious hills, another surprise.

The ride begins at the Top Rock Trail parking area for State Game Lands 157, the largest of the state game lands in Bucks County with 2,011 acres covering most of Haycock Mountain. To get there, turn onto Top Rock Trail from Route 563. The unpaved parking lot is 0.6 miles ahead on the left, just before the road makes a sharp turn to the right. Parking here allows you to start this ride in one of its quietest and prettiest sections as it follows Haycock Run.

A noteworthy site on the route is the Sheard's Mill Covered Bridge, aptly situated on Covered Bridge Road. This bridge, which has a white front and red sides, was built in 1873.

Two variations on the route provide shorter rides in the area. Both of these variations begin at the game lands parking area near the entrance to the rifle range on Saw Mill Road. Saw Mill doesn't intersect Route 563 but instead passes under it, so use Harrisburg School Road, Cedar Lane, and Saw Mill to reach the parking area from Route 563.

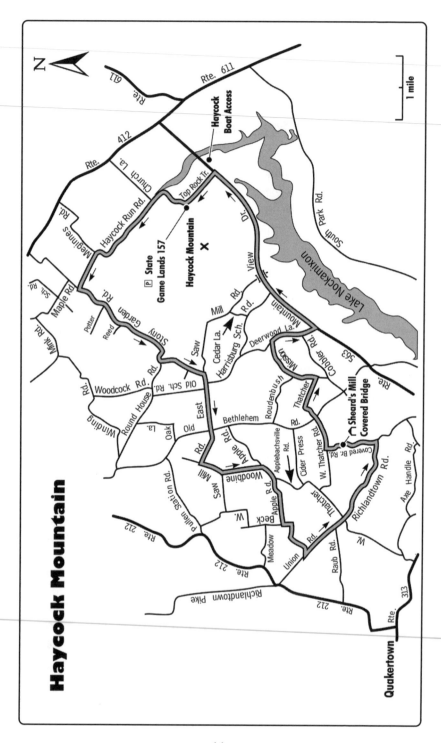

Haycock Mountain

Haycock Mountain

P		**Game Lands 157 parking area, Top Rock Tr., Haycock Twp.**
0.0	L	Top Rock Trail
0.4	L	Haycock Run Rd.
2.6	L	Stony Garden Rd.
5.3	R	E. Saw Mill Rd.
6.2	X	Old Bethlehem Rd.
7.1	L	Woodbine La
7.8	R	Apple Rd.
8.8	L	Beck Rd.
9.6	L	Union Rd.
10.4	X	W. Thatcher Rd.
	S	Richlandtown Rd.
11.8	L	Covered Bridge Rd.
12.7	R	W. Thatcher Rd.
13.2	X	Old Bethlehem Rd.
14.0	L	Mission Rd.
15.0	R	Deerwood La.
15.8	L	Mountain View Dr./Rte. 563
18.9	L	Top Rock Trail
19.6	L	Return to game lands parking area

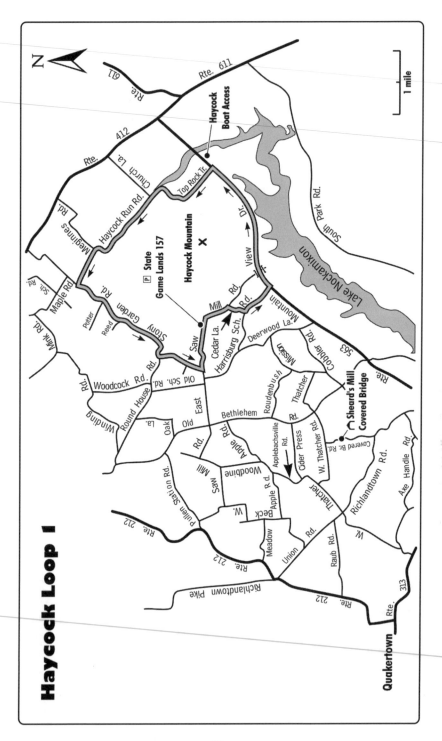

Haycock Loop 1

Haycock Loop I

P   **Game Lands 157 parking area,**
   E. Saw Mill Rd., Haycock Twp.

0.0	L	E. Saw Mill Rd.
0.6	R	Cedar La.
0.9	L	Harrisburg School Rd.
1.5	L	Mountain View Rd./Rte. 563
3.7	L	Top Rock Trail
4.8	L	Haycock Run Rd.
7.0	L	Stony Garden Rd.
9.7	L	E. Saw Mill Rd.
10.2	L	Return to game lands parking area

Haycock Loop 2

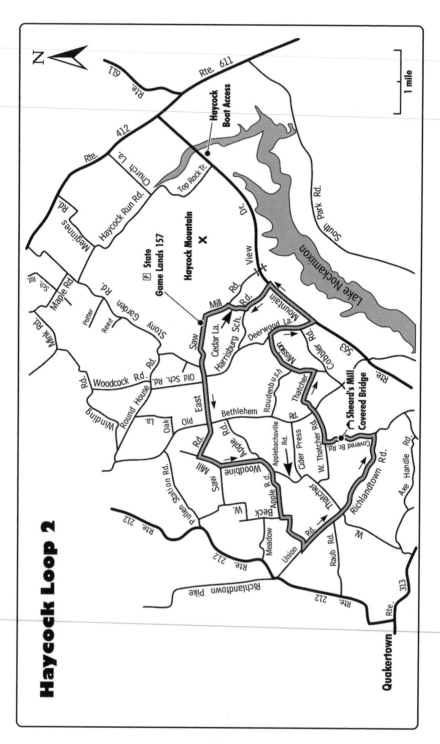

Haycock Loop 2

P		Game Lands 157 parking area, E. Saw Mill Rd., Haycock Twp.
0.0	R	E. Saw Mill Rd.
1.5	X	Old Bethlehem Rd.
2.4	L	Woodbine Rd.
3.1	R	Apple Rd.
4.1	L	Beck Rd.
4.9	L	Union Rd.
5.7	X	W. Thatcher Rd.
	S	Richlandtown Rd.
7.1	L	Covered Bridge Rd.
8.0	R	W. Thatcher Rd.
8.5	X	Old Bethlehem Rd.
9.3	L	Mission Rd.
10.3	R	Deerwood La.
11.1	L	Mountain View Rd./Rte. 563
12.0	L	Harrisburg Sch. Rd.
12.6	R	Cedar La.
12.9	L	E. Saw Mill Rd.
13.5	R	Return to game lands parking area

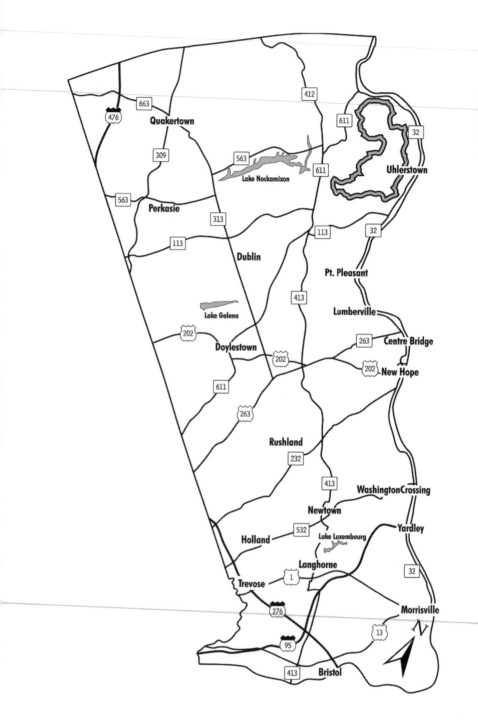

Ringing Rocks

Distance: 24.1 miles

Start: Ringing Rocks Park
              Ringing Rocks Rd., Bridgetown Twp.

Terrain: Rolling country roads with a few hills; 1 mile
              unpaved

Variations: 8.2 miles on rolling country roads

Ringing Rocks Park is one of Buck's County's more unusual attractions. A short foot trail from the parking area leads to an imposing sight: an eight-acre field of large boulders piled several deep. Many of these boulders ring like bells when struck with a hammer. You might wonder how anyone ever discovered this, but the ones that ring best are easy to find now because they're marked with worn spots from many hammer blows.

Similar rocks are scattered across much of the landscape in this remote and somewhat isolated part of Bucks County. The area also seems to have disproportionate numbers of barking dogs and what one might be tempted to call mobile homes, except that it's clear they won't be moving anytime soon.

It also has some lovely scenery. Sheep Hole Road is a mile of unpaved road following Tinicum Creek through an isolated valley. Lake Warren is a treasure hidden by trees from cars passing on Kintner Hill and Lake Warren Roads. Geigel Hill Road offers sweeping views of distant hills.

There are hills on the ride, too, but nothing severe. Upper Tinicum Church Road climbs for several miles, but it isn't too steep. Geigel Hill is steep and winding as it heads down toward Sheep Hole. The shorter variation avoids both of these places, though it does include several small hills.

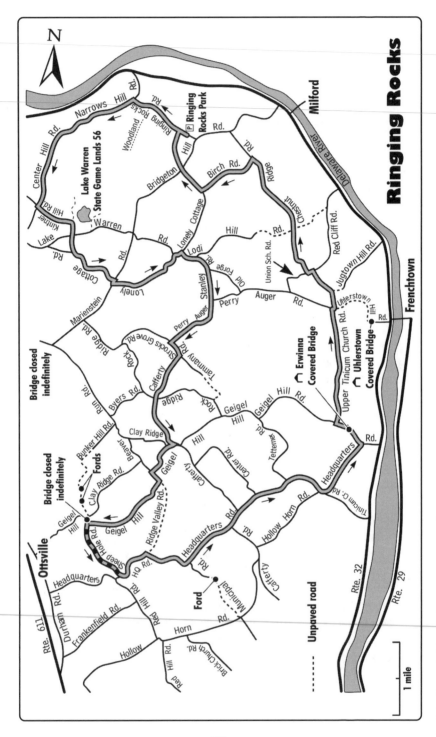

Ringing Rocks

Ringing Rocks

<table>
<tr><td>P</td><td></td><td>Ringing Rocks Park,
Ringing Rocks Rd., BridgetonTwp.</td></tr>
<tr><td>0.0</td><td>R</td><td>Ringing Rocks Rd.</td></tr>
<tr><td>1.3</td><td>L</td><td>Narrows Hill Rd.
BECOMES CENTER HILL RD.</td></tr>
<tr><td>3.2</td><td>L</td><td>Kintner Hill Rd.</td></tr>
<tr><td>4.1</td><td>S</td><td>Lonely Cottage Rd.</td></tr>
<tr><td>4.5</td><td>L</td><td>Lonely Cottage Rd.</td></tr>
<tr><td>5.0</td><td>R</td><td>Marienstein Rd.</td></tr>
<tr><td>5.0</td><td>L</td><td>Lonely Cottage Rd.</td></tr>
<tr><td>6.0</td><td>R</td><td>Lonely Cottage Rd.</td></tr>
<tr><td>6.2</td><td>R</td><td>Lodi Hill Rd.</td></tr>
<tr><td>6.4</td><td>R</td><td>Old Forge Rd.
LODI HILL RD. GOES LEFT</td></tr>
<tr><td>6.6</td><td>R</td><td>Stanley Rd.</td></tr>
<tr><td>7.1</td><td>S</td><td>Perry Auger Rd.</td></tr>
<tr><td>8.0</td><td>L</td><td>Tammany Rd.
STROCKS GROVE RD. GOES RIGHT</td></tr>
<tr><td>8.2</td><td>R</td><td>Cafferty Rd.</td></tr>
<tr><td>9.7</td><td>R</td><td>Geigel Hill Rd.</td></tr>
<tr><td>11.8</td><td>L</td><td>Sheep Hole Rd.</td></tr>
<tr><td>12.7</td><td>L</td><td>Headquarters Rd.</td></tr>
<tr><td>16.5</td><td>L</td><td>Headquarters Rd.
TINICUM CREEK RD. GOES STRAIGHT</td></tr>
<tr><td>17.4</td><td>L</td><td>Geigel Hill Rd.</td></tr>
<tr><td>17.5</td><td>X</td><td>Covered bridge</td></tr>
<tr><td>17.9</td><td>R</td><td>Upper Tinicum Church Rd.</td></tr>
<tr><td>19.5</td><td>S</td><td>Upper Tinicum Church Rd.
TAKE THE MIDDLE OF THREE ROADS</td></tr>
<tr><td>20.2</td><td>L</td><td>Upper Tinicum Church Rd.
RED CLIFF RD. ON RIGHT</td></tr>
<tr><td>20.2</td><td>R</td><td>Upper Tinicum Church Rd.
UNION SCHOOL RD. AHEAD;
UNPAVED TRIANGLE IN MIDDLE</td></tr>
<tr><td>20.9</td><td>X</td><td>Lodi Hill Rd.</td></tr>
<tr><td></td><td>S</td><td>Chestnut Ridge Rd.</td></tr>
<tr><td>22.1</td><td>L</td><td>Birch Rd.</td></tr>
<tr><td>23.0</td><td>R</td><td>Lonely Cottage Rd.</td></tr>
<tr><td>23.4</td><td>X</td><td>Bridgetown Hill Rd.</td></tr>
<tr><td>24.0</td><td>R</td><td>Ringing Rocks Rd.</td></tr>
<tr><td>24.1</td><td>L</td><td>Return to Ringing
Rocks Park</td></tr>
</table>

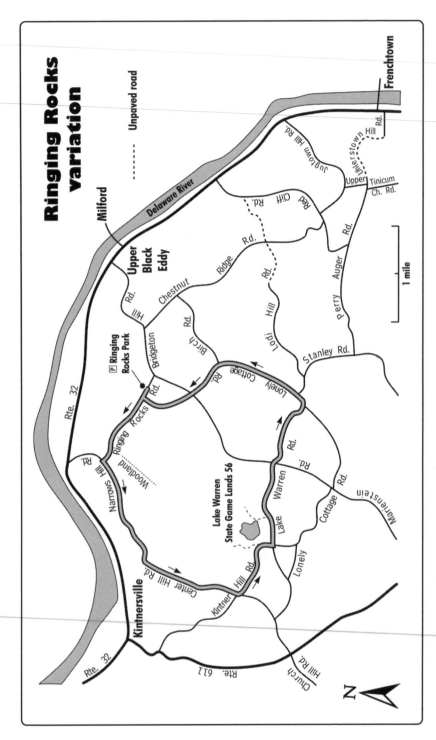

Ringing Rocks variation

.... Unpaved road

Milford

Upper Black Eddy

Delaware River

Frenchtown

1 mile

Rte. 32

P Ringing Rocks Park

Chestnut Hill Rd.

Bridgeton Rd.

Birch Rd.

Ridge Rd.

Lodi Hill Rd.

Red Cliff Rd.

Jugtown Hill Rd.

Uhlerstown Hill Rd.

Upper Tinicum Ch. Rd.

Perry Auger Rd.

Stanley Rd.

Lonely Cottage Rd.

Ringing Rocks Rd.

Narrows Hill Rd.

Woodland Rd.

Lake Warren
State Game Lands 56

Lake Warren Rd.

Cottage Rd.

Martenstein

Lonely Rd.

Kintner Hill Rd.

Center Hill Rd.

Kintnersville

Rte. 32

Rte. 611

Church Hill Rd.

N

Ringing Rocks variation

P Ringing Rocks Park,
    Ringing Rocks Rd., Bridgeton Twp.

0.0 R Ringing Rocks Rd.

0.9 L Narrows Hill Rd.
BECOMES CENTER HILL RD.

3.2 L Kintner Hill Rd.

4.0 L Lake Warren Rd.

5.0 X Marienstein Rd.

6.0 L Lonely Cottage Rd.

7.5 X Bridgeton Hill Rd.

8.1 R Ringing Rocks Rd.

8.2 L Return to Ringing
    Rocks Park

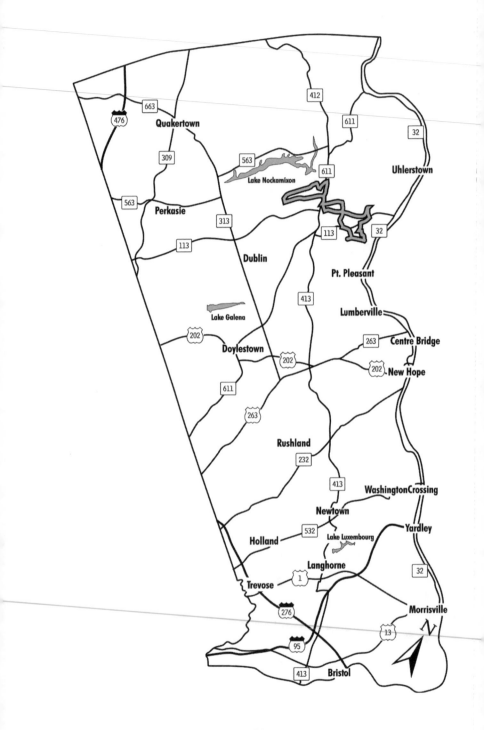

Ottsville

Distance: 20.0 miles

Start: High Rocks parking area, Ralph Stover State Park
Tory Road, Tinicum Township

Terrain: Country roads; hilly, with a very steep downhill
approaching the covered bridge; 0.4 miles unpaved

Variations: 13.5 and 11.8 miles on hilly country roads

This route includes two different types of countryside. West of Route 611, a large area of open farmland is mostly flat with a few steep hills. On the east side of 611, the landscape is wooded and quite hilly throughout.

The parking lot for the High Rocks area of Ralph Stover State Park is the starting point for two of the three versions of the ride. High Rocks, a 200-foot cliff above Tohickon Creek, is a favorite with rock climbers. A short walk through the woods across Tory Road from the parking area leads to the edge of the cliff, where you can enjoy a sweeping view of surrounding woodlands.

The third ride, Ottsville Loop 2, begins on South Park Road in a small parking lot that is part of Nockamixon State Park. This lot is poorly marked; look for it a little west of the Nockamixon dam, another interesting landmark.

The Frankenfield Covered bridge is just off the route but clearly visible when you reach the bottom of the steep hill on Caffery Road. The bridge, built in 1872, makes a pleasant place to stop for a break.

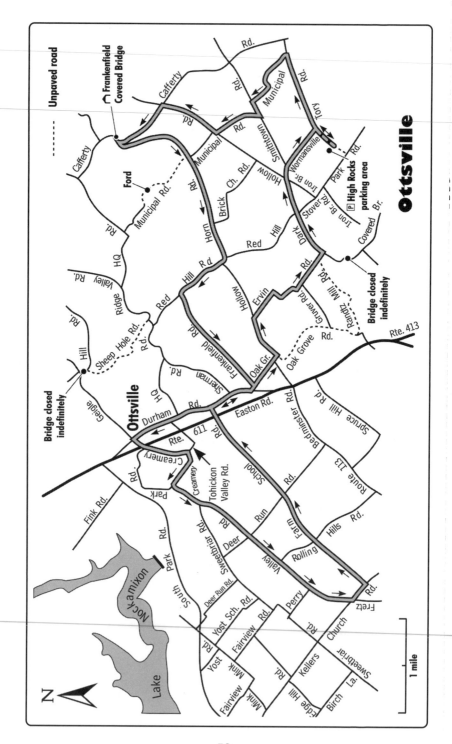

Ottsville

P		High Rocks parking area, Tory Rd., Tinicum Twp.
0.0	L	Tory Rd.
1.1	L	Municipal Rd.
1.8	L	Smithtown Rd.
2.0	R	Municipal Rd.
2.5	R	Dark Hollow Rd.
3.2	L	Cafferty Rd.
3.9	L	Hollow Horn Rd.
		FRANKENFIELD BRIDGE TO RIGHT
6.0	R	Red Hill Rd.
6.6	L	Frankenfield Rd.
8.0	R	Oak Grove Rd.
8.0	R	Durham Rd.
9.4	L	Creamery Rd.
9.5	L	Creamery Rd.
10.1	R	Creamery Rd.
10.5	L	Creamery Rd.
10.8	L	Fretz Valley Rd.
12.8	L	Kellers Church Rd.
13.0	L	Farm School Rd.
15.5	X	Rte. 611/Easton Rd.
15.6	R	Durham Rd.
16.2	L	Oak Grove Rd.
16.6	L	Hollow Horn Rd.
17.1	R	Ervin Rd.
18.2	L	Dark Hollow Rd.
19.1	BR	Smithtown Rd.
19.3	R	Wormansville Rd.
19.8	R	Tory Rd.
20.0	R	Return to High Rocks parking area

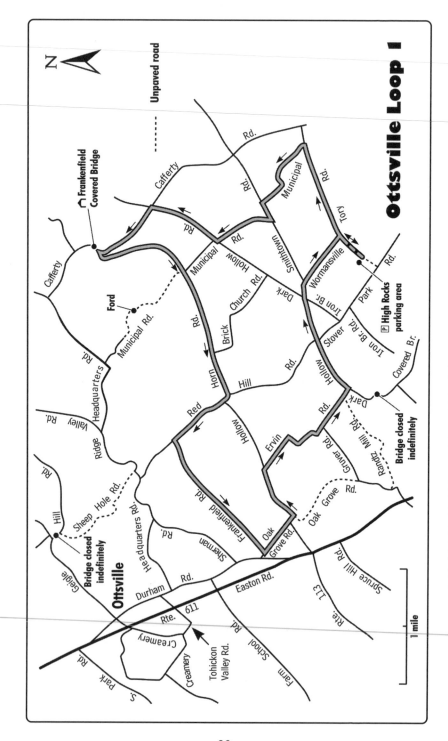

Ottsville Loop 1

Frankenfield Covered Bridge

Unpaved road

N

Ford

High Rocks parking area

Bridge closed indefinitely

Bridge closed indefinitely

Ottsville

1 mile

Cafferty Rd.
Municipal Rd.
Tory Rd.
Wormansville
Park Rd.
Iron Br. Rd.
Covered Br.
Stover Rd.
Dark Hollow Rd.
Randtz Mill Rd.
Gruver Rd.
Oak Grove Rd.
Erwin Rd.
Red Horn Rd.
Hill Hollow
Brick Church Rd.
Dark Hollow
Smithtown
Municipal Rd.
Cafferty Rd.
Headquarters Rd.
Ridge Valley Rd.
Sheep Hole Rd.
Geigle Rd.
Hill Rd.
S. Park Rd.
Creamery Rd.
Tohickon Valley Rd.
Rte. 611
Durham Rd.
Sherman Rd.
Headquarters Rd.
Frankenfield Rd.
Oak Grove Rd.
Easton Rd.
Farm School Rd.
Spruce Hill Rd.
Rte. 113

Ottsville Loop I

P   **High Rocks parking area, Tory Rd., Tinicum Twp.**

0.0	L	Tory Rd.
1.1	L	Municipal Rd.
1.8	L	Smithtown Rd.
2.0	R	Municipal Rd.
2.5	R	Dark Hollow Rd.
3.2	L	Cafferty Rd.
3.8	L	Hollow Horn Rd.
		FRANKENFIELD BRIDGE TO RIGHT
6.1	R	Red Hill Rd.
6.6	L	Frankenfield Rd.
8.0	L	Oak Grove Rd.
8.4	L	Hollow Horn Rd.
8.9	R	Ervin Rd.
10.0	L	Dark Hollow Rd.
11.0	BR	Smithtown Rd.
11.1	R	Wormansville Rd.
11.6	R	Tory Rd.
11.8	R	Return to High Rocks parking area

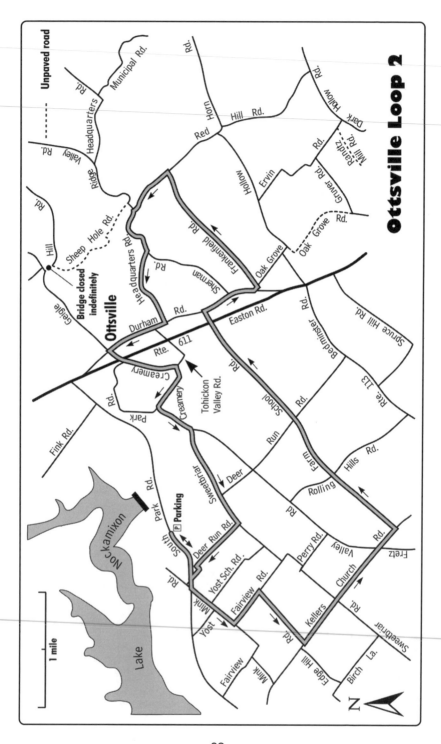

Ottsville Loop 2

Ottsville Loop 2

P   **Nockamixon State Park,**
South Park Rd., Bedminster Twp.

0.0	L	South Park Rd.
0.6	L	Mink Rd.
1.1	L	Fairview Rd.
1.4	R	Edge Hill Rd.
2.0	L	Keller's Church Rd.
3.3	L	Farm School Rd.
5.7	X	Easton Rd.
5.8	R	Durham Rd.
6.3	L	Oak Grove Rd.
6.4	L	Frankenfield Rd.
7.7	L	Red Hill Rd.
8.2	L	Headquarters Rd.
9.3	R	Durham Rd.
9.9	L	Creamery Rd.
10.0	L	Creamery Rd.
10.6	R	Creamery Rd.
11.0	L	Creamery Rd.
11.3	R	Sweetbriar Rd.
12.3	R	Deer Run Rd.
13.0	R	South Park Rd.
13.5	R	Return to parking area

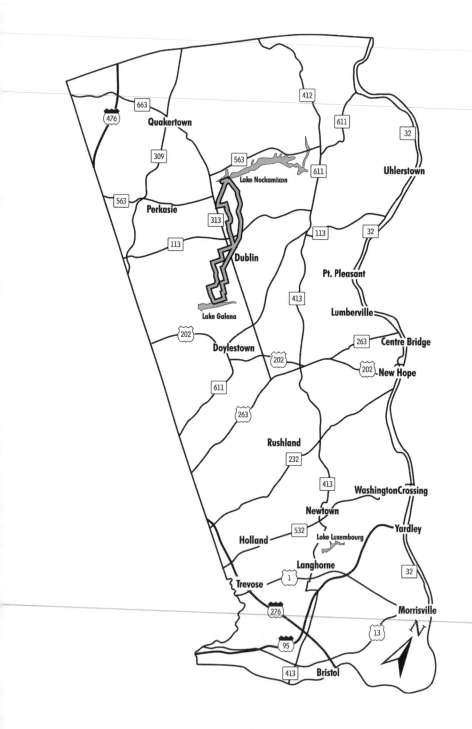

Lake to Lake

Distance:	19.6 miles
Start:	Peace Valley Park, main entrance
	New Galena Road, New Britain Township
Terrain:	Country roads; hilly, especially near lakes
Variations:	9.5 and 10.1 miles on hilly country roads;
	11.5 miles on rolling country roads

Some of the prettiest scenery in Bucks County isn't natural in the strict sense of the word.

Lake Galena and Lake Nockamixon were both created by damming creeks to create reservoirs. Both are surrounded by parkland, and both have paved multi-use paths that offer easy riding and great scenery. (See pages 8 and 16 for more information about these parks.)

For those who prefer more challenging cycling, this ride between the two lakes is a good bet. The land between the lakes includes wide areas of undisturbed farmland, although development there is on the rise. This middle ground is also relatively flat, although there are long, steep hills approaching each of the lakes and another steep hill just after the turn onto Old Bethlehem Pike. (If you don't wish to stop at Lake Nockamixon, you can bypass the last part of the final hill there by riding across West Creek Road.)

The two optional loops offer shorter versions of the lake-to-lake route, but they don't avoid the hills. However, most of the Dublin area is fairly flat, so the ride around that borough is a relatively easy route.

Several warnings are in order: Watch out for the open grate bridge at the bottom of the hill on Keller Road, and be prepared for the stop sign at the bottom of the long hill on Old Limekiln Road near Lake Galena at the end of the ride.

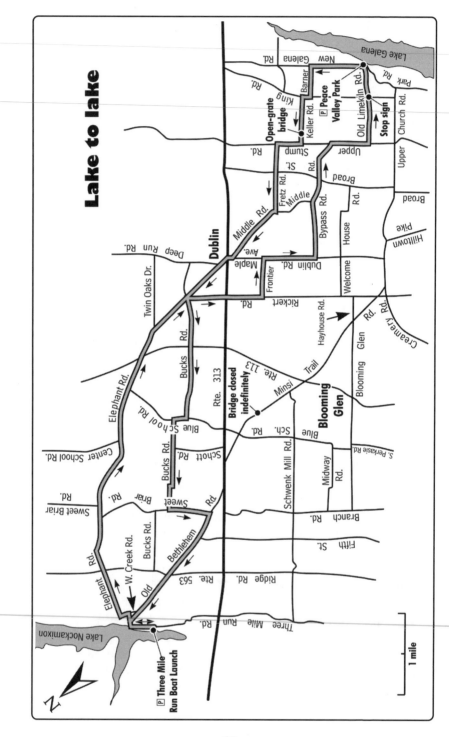

Lake to lake

Lake to lake

Mile	Dir	Location
P		Peace Valley Park, main entrance, New Galena Rd., New Britain Twp.
0.0	R	New Galena Rd.
0.6	L	Barner Rd.
1.0	R	King Rd.
1.1	L	Keller Rd.
		‼ WATCH FOR OPEN-GRATE BRIDGE AT BOTTOM OF HILL
1.7	R	Upper Stump Rd.
2.0	L	Fretz Rd.
2.8	R	Middle Rd.
3.6	R	Maple Ave.
3.7	X	Rte. 313
	S	Elephant Rd.
4.4	L	Bucks Rd.
5.9	R	Blue School Rd.
6.1	L	Bucks Rd.
7.2	L	Sweet Briar Rd.
7.7	R	Old Bethlehem Pike
8.7	X	Ridge Rd.
9.4	L	Elephant Rd.
9.5	L	Three Mile Run Rd.
9.7	R	parking area TURN AROUND AND GO BACK
9.9	R	Elephant Rd.
10.8	X	Ridge Rd.
13.5	X	Rte. 113
14.5	R	Rickert Rd.
15.0	X	Rte. 313
15.5	L	Frontier Rd.
16.0	R	Dublin Rd.
16.7	L	Bypass Rd.
17.3	S	Middle Rd.
17.6	X	Broad St.
18.1	R	Upper Stump Rd.
18.6	L	Old Limekiln Rd.
		‼ WATCH FOR STOP SIGN AT BOTTOM OF HILL
19.6	R	Return to Peace Valley parking area

Lake Loop 1

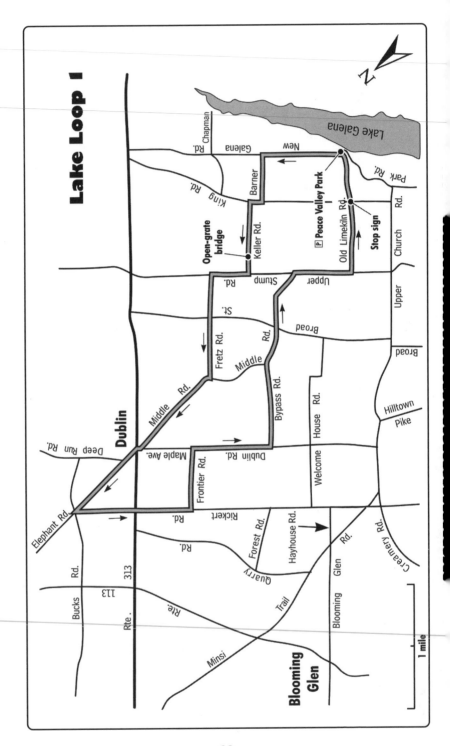

Lake Loop I

P		Peace Valley Park, main entrance, New Galena Rd., New Britain Twp.
0.0	R	New Galena Rd.
0.6	L	Barner Rd.
1.0	R	King Rd.
1.1	L	Keller Rd.
	!	WATCH FOR OPEN-GRATE BRIDGE AT BOTTOM OF HILL
1.7	R	Upper Stump Rd.
2.0	L	Fretz Rd.
2.8	R	Middle Rd.
3.6	R	Maple Ave.
3.7	X	Rte. 313
	S	Elephant Rd.
4.4	L	Rickert Rd.
4.9	X	Rte. 313
5.4	L	Frontier Rd.
5.9	R	Dublin Rd.
6.5	L	Bypass Rd.
7.2	S	Middle Rd.
7.5	X	Broad St.
8.0	R	Upper Stump Rd.
8.5	L	Old Limekiln Rd.
	!	WATCH FOR STOP SIGN AT BOTTOM OF HILL
9.5	R	Return to Peace Valley parking area

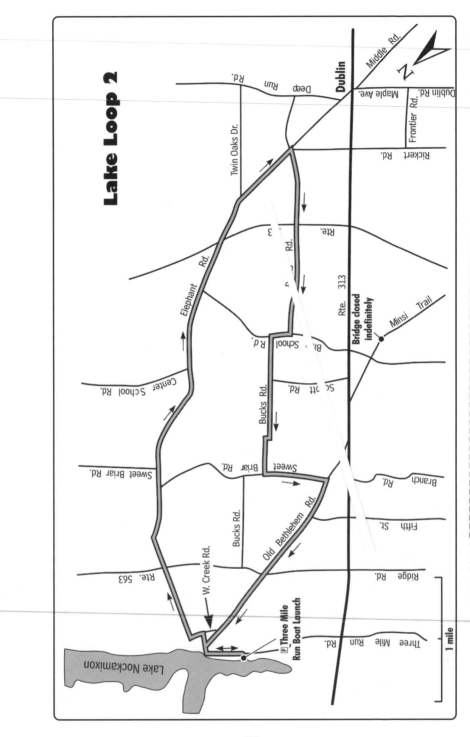

Lake Loop 2

Lake Nockamixon

Three Mile Run Boat Launch

Bridge closed indefinitely

Dublin

Middle Rd.
Maple Ave.
Dublin Rd.
Frontier Rd.
Rickert Rd.
Deep Run Rd.
Twin Oaks Dr.
Rte. 313
Minsi Trail
School Rd.
Scott Rd.
Bucks Rd.
Branch Rd.
Fifth St.
Sweet Briar Rd.
Center School Rd.
Elephant Rd.
Old Bethlehem Rd.
W. Creek Rd.
Bucks Rd.
Rte. 563
Ridge Rd.
Three Mile Run Rd.

1 mile

Lake Loop 2

P **Nockamixon State Park,
Three Mile Run Boat Launch,
Three Mile Run Rd., E. Rockhill Twp.**

0.0	L	Three Mile Run Rd.
0.2	R	Elephant Rd.
1.0	X	Rte. 563
3.8	X	Rte. 113
4.8	R	Bucks Rd.
5.4	X	Rte. 113
6.3	R	Blue School Rd.
6.5	L	Bucks Rd.
7.6	L	Sweet Briar Rd.
8.1	R	Old Bethlehem Pike
9.0	X	Rte. 563
9.8	L	Elephant Rd.
9.9	L	Three Mile Run Rd.
10.1	R	Return to Three Mile Run Rd. parking area

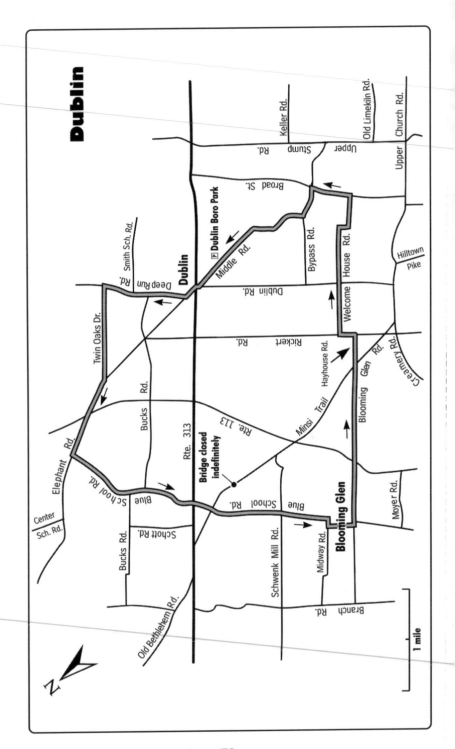

Dublin

Keller Rd.
Old Limekiln Rd.
Upper Church Rd.
Upper
Stump Rd.
Broad St.
Bypass Rd.
P Dublin Boro Park
Hilltown Pike
Smith Sch. Rd.
Dublin
Deep Run Rd.
Middle Rd.
Welcome House Rd.
Dublin Rd.
Twin Oaks Dr.
Rickert Rd.
Creamery Rd.
Blooming Glen Rd.
Bucks Rd.
Minsi Trail
Hayhouse Rd.
Elephant Rd.
Rte. 313
Rte. 113
Bridge closed indefinitely
Blue School Rd.
Moyer Rd.
Center Sch. Rd.
Schott Rd.
Blue School Rd.
Blooming Glen
Bucks Rd.
Midway Rd.
Schwenk Mill Rd.
Branch Rd.
Old Bethlehem Rd.

N

1 mile

Dublin

P		Dublin Borough Park, Middle Rd., Dublin Boro
0.0	R	Middle Rd.
0.2	R	Maple Ave.
0.2	X	Rte. 313
	S	Elephant Rd.
0.3	R	Deep Run Rd.
1.2	L	Twin Oaks Dr.
2.2	S	Elephant Rd.
3.0	L	Blue School Rd.
4.4	X	Rte. 313
⚠		NO LIGHT; WATCH FOR TRAFFIC
6.0	L	Blooming Glen Rd.
	X	Minsi Trail
7.7	S	Hayhouse Rd.
8.0	L	Rickert Rd.
8.1	R	Welcome House Rd.
9.6	L	Broad St.
10.0	L	Middle Rd.
10.3	R	Middle Rd.
11.5	R	Return to Dublin Borough Park

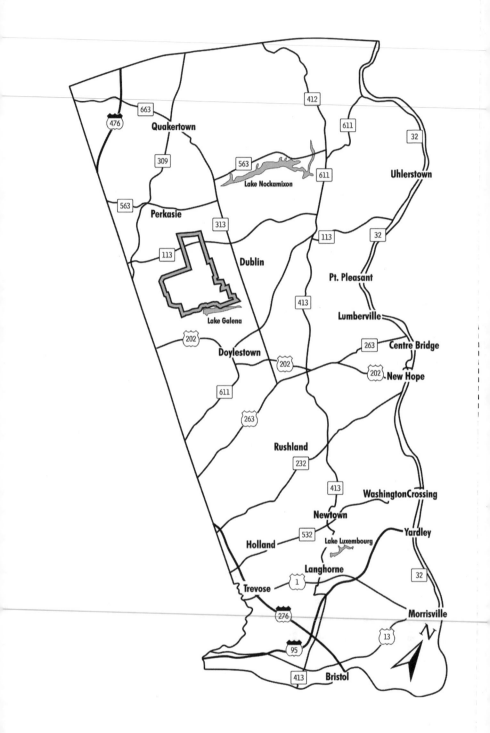

Hilltown

Distance: 18.0 miles
Start: Sailors' Point parking area, Peace Valley Park
                Park Road, New Britain Township
Terrain: Country roads, with some hills on southern loop
Variations: 14.0 miles on hilly roads; 6.6 miles on rolling roads

It hasn't escaped the proliferation of new development that sometimes seems to be swallowing Bucks County's open spaces, but Hilltown Township still has some of the most rural landscapes in Bucks County, with wide expanses of gently rolling farmland and views of Haycock Mountain in the distance.

This ride begins on the shores of Lake Galena in New Britain Township but soon moves into Hilltown. There are a few hills on the route, but they aren't nearly as bad as the name *Hilltown* might suggest. In fact, for long stretches the land is nearly level. The toughest hills come near the start of the ride, as you climb away from Lake Galena in Peace Valley Park. After that, some of the steepest inclines go downhill rather than up.

The route includes about a tenth of a mile on Hilltown Pike, a heavily traveled road that merits extra caution.

One of the prettiest views lies behind you if you follow the prescribed route. Be sure to turn around and admire the scenery on Telegraph Road as you approach Rickert Road.

For those who prefer a short, relatively easy ride, the variation beginning at the Blooming Glen Playground avoids the worst hills. The playground is located in a corner of land between Route 133 and Blooming Glen Road, and parking can be reached from either street. To find it from Blooming Glen Road, go behind the former Hilltown High School building across from the Blooming Glen Post Office.

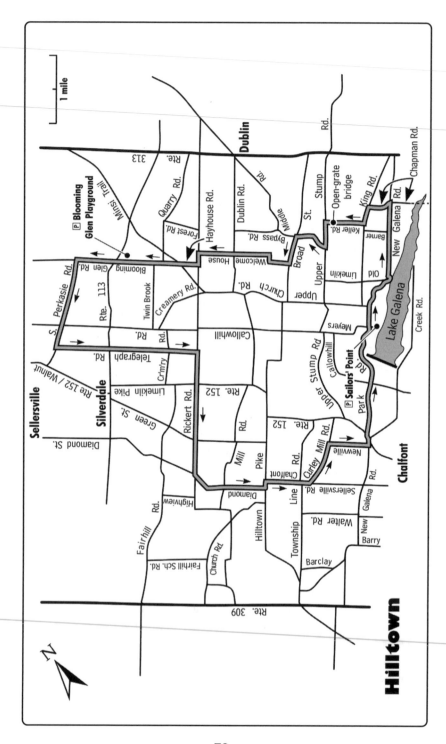

Hilltown

P		Sailors' Point parking area, Peace Valley Park Park Rd., New Britain Twp.
0.0	R	Park Rd.
0.9	R	New Galena Rd.
1.9	L	Chapman Rd.
2.3	L	King Rd.
2.5	R	Keller Rd.
		❢ WATCH FOR OPEN-GRATE BRIDGE AT BOTTOM OF HILL
3.1	L	Upper Stump Rd.
3.5	R	Middle Rd.
4.0	L	Broad St.
4.4	R	Welcome House Rd.
5.9	L	Rickert Rd.
6.0	R	Hayhouse Rd.
6.4	X	Minsi Trail
7.3	S	Blooming Glen Rd.
7.3	X	Rte. 113
7.9	L	S. Perkasie Rd.
9.2	L	Telegraph Rd.
11.3	R	Rickert Rd.
13.1	L	Diamond St.
14.3	L	Hilltown Pike
		❢ WATCH FOR TRAFFIC
14.4	R	Chalfont Rd.
15.0	L	Curley Mill Rd.
15.7	R	Newville Rd.
16.3	L	New Galena Rd.
16.4	L	Rte. 152/Limekiln Pike
16.4	R	New Galena Rd.
17.2	X	Callowhill Rd.
	S	Park Rd.
18.0	R	Return to Sailors' Point parking area

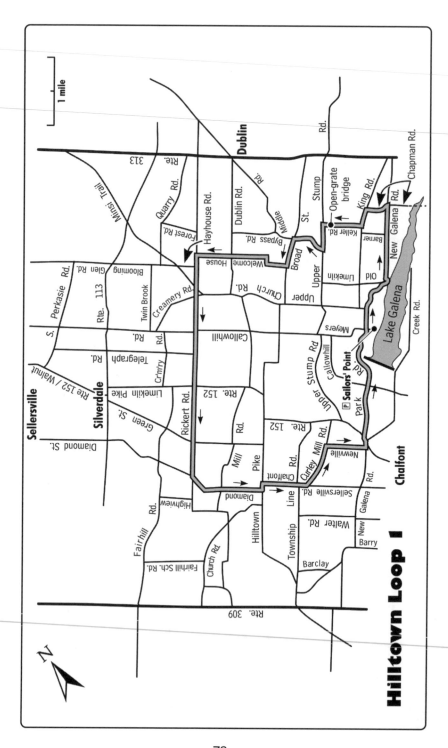

Hilltown Loop I

Hilltown Loop I

P Sailors' Point parking area, Peace Valley Park

0.0	R	Park Rd.
0.9	R	New Galena Rd.
1.9	L	Chapman Rd.
2.3	L	King Rd.
2.5	R	Keller Rd.

❢ WATCH FOR OPEN-GRATE BRIDGE AT BOTTOM OF HILL

3.1	L	Upper Stump Rd.
3.5	R	Middle Rd.
4.0	L	Broad St.
4.4	R	Welcome House Rd.
5.9	L	Rickert Rd.
9.1	L	Diamond St.
10.2	L	Hilltown Pike
10.3	R	Chalfont Rd.

11.0	L	Curley Mill Rd.
11.6	R	Newville Rd.
12.2	L	New Galena Rd.
12.3	L	Rte. 152/Likekiln Pike
12.3	R	New Galena Rd.
13.1	X	Callowhill Rd.
	S	Park Rd.
14.0	R	Return to Sailors' Point parking area

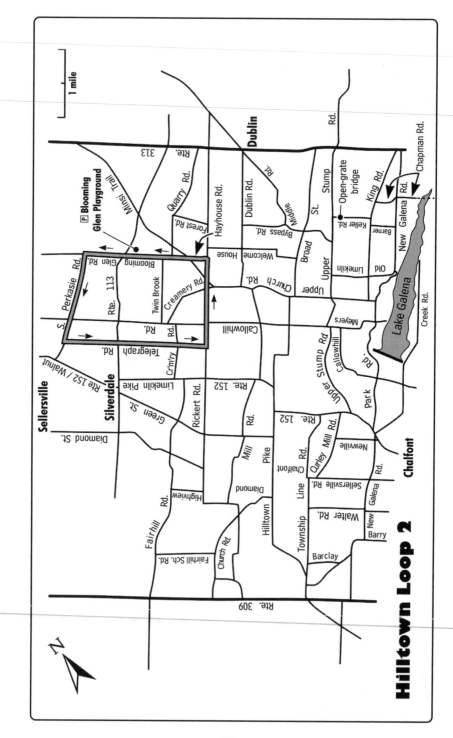

Hilltown Loop 2

Hilltown Loop 2

P **Blooming Glen Playground,**
Blooming Glen Rd., Blooming Glen

0.0 R Blooming Glen Rd.

0.1 X Rte. 113

0.6 L S. Perkasie Rd.

2.0 L Telegraph Rd.

2.8 X Rte. 113

4.1 L Rickert Rd.

5.4 L Hayhouse Rd.

5.7 X Minsi Trail

S Blooming Glen Rd.

6.6 R Return to
Blooming Glen Playground

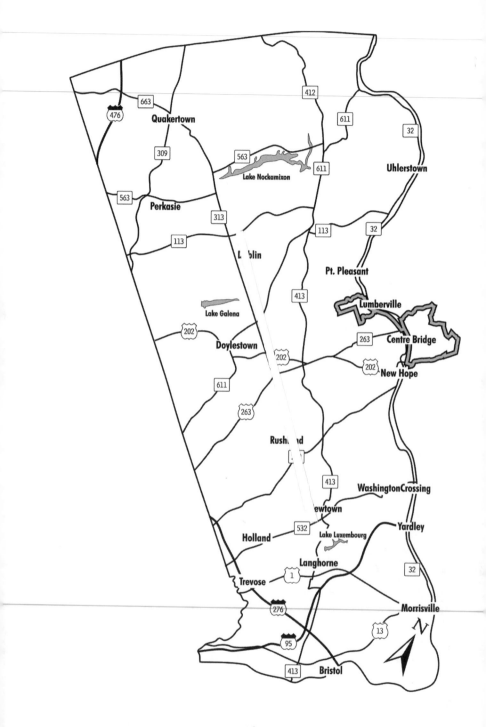

Centre Bridge

Distance: 26.1 miles

Start: Virginia Forrest Recreation Area,
Route 32, Solebury Township

Terrain: A mix of roads with some hills; 1 mile on unpaved
road; 8.2 miles on towpath

Variations: 9.7 and 16.7 miles as above, longer loop is hillier;
4.6 miles on gently rolling country road

The Virginia Forrest Recreation Area is an ideal starting point for biking the Delaware Canal towpath and for rides like these, which use the towpath to reach back roads with no public parking nearby. Located on Route 32 just north of Centre Bridge, Pa., the recreation area consists of a few picnic tables, some restrooms, and a large parking lot right next to the canal. (See page 3 for more about riding the towpath.)

The Pennsylvania part of this ride goes north along the towpath to the town of Lumberville, where it turns onto Fleecydale Road—a favorite with cyclists—for a gentle climb to the town of Carversville. From there it goes on to Cuttalossa Road, another scenic favorite, and descends back to the river.

In New Jersey, the route goes south to Lambertville, where it turns inland. Like Fleecydale, Alexauken Road provides an easy and pretty climb out of the river valley. This ride includes a lot of pleasant scenery, but the sweeping view from Covered Bridge Road just before the downhill to Lower Creek Road is a special treat. Lower Creek Road, which follows the Wickecheoke Creek back out of the woods, is another favorite with cyclists.

The Fleecydale variation is a short, easy ride that can be lengthened by continuing along the canal. Limited parking is available next to Lock No. 12 in Lumberville, with more across the Delaware River at Bull's Island Recreation Area. Both Lumberville and Carversville have stores where you can buy refreshments.

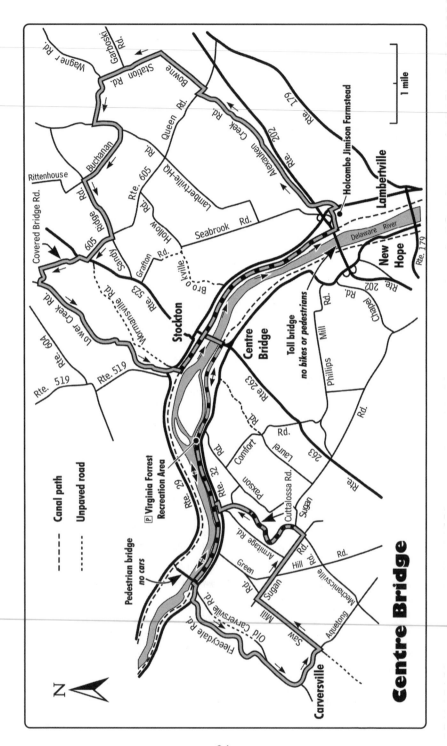

Centre Bridge

Legend:
- - - - Canal path
·········· Unpaved road

P Virginia Forrest Recreation Area

Pedestrian bridge *no cars*

Toll bridge *no bikes or pedestrians*

N

1 mile

Holcombe Jimison Farmstead

Lambertville

New Hope

Delaware River

Rte. 179

Rte. 202

Alexauken Creek Rd.

Rte. 29

Queen Rd.

Bowne Station Rd.

Garboski Rd.

Wagner Rd.

Rittenhouse

Buchanan Rd.

Ridge Rd.

Covered Bridge Rd.

Rte. 605

Lambertville-HQ Rd.

Hollow Rd.

Seabrook Rd.

Grafton Rd.

Brookville

Rte. 523

Sandy

Womansville Rd.

Stockton

Rte. 519

Rte. 519

Rte. 604

Lower Creek Rd.

Centre Bridge

Rte. 263

Rte. 32

Rte. 29

Comfort Rd.

Laurel Rd.

Rte. 263

Cuttalossa Rd.

Paxson

Sugan

Rte. 263

Phillips Rd.

Mill Rd.

Chapel Rd.

Rte. 202

Rte. 179

Armitage Rd.

Green

Sugan

Hill Rd.

Mechanicsville Rd.

Aquetong Rd.

Saw Mill Rd.

Old Carversville Rd.

Fleecydale Rd.

Carversville

84

Centre Bridge

📄 **Virginia Forrest Recreation Area, Rte. 32, Solebury Twp.**

0.0	R	Towpath
		RIDE NORTH
2.0	L	Cross the canal using the bridge in Lumberville
	R	Rte. 32
2.2	L	Fleecydale Rd.
4.2	S	Aquetong Rd.
4.8	L	Saw Mill Rd.
5.8	R	Sugan Rd.
6.8	L	Sugan Rd.
7.0	L	Cuttalossa Rd.
8.4	R	Rte. 32
8.5	L	Bridge over canal at Delaware Quarries
8.5	R	Towpath
10.6	L	Carry bike up stairs from towpath
	R	Bridge to N.J.
10.8	R	Delaware & Raritan Canal path
13.2	L	Driveway to Holcombe Jimison Farmstead
		JUST PAST RTE. 202 TOLL BRIDGE
13.4	R	Rte. 29
13.5	L	Alexauken Creek Rd.
15.8	R	Queen Rd.
15.9	L	Bowne Station Rd.
18.1	L	Lambertville-Headquarters Rd.
18.5	R	Buchanan Rd.
19.4	L	Sandy Ridge Rd.
20.3	R	Rte. 605
20.6	R	Rte. 523
20.7	L	Covered Bridge Rd.
		❗ WATCH FOR TURNS AT BOTTOM OF HILL
21.5	L	Lower Creek Rd.
23.6	L	Rte. 519
23.7	S	Rte. 29
24.0	R	Enter Prallsville Mills
		FOLLOW DRIVE TO CANAL PATH BEHIND MILL BUILDINGS
24.1	L	Towpath
24.4	R	Bridge St.
	X	Bridge to Pa.
24.7	L	Carry bike down stairs to towpath
	R	Towpath
26.1	R	Return to Virginia Forrest Recreation Area

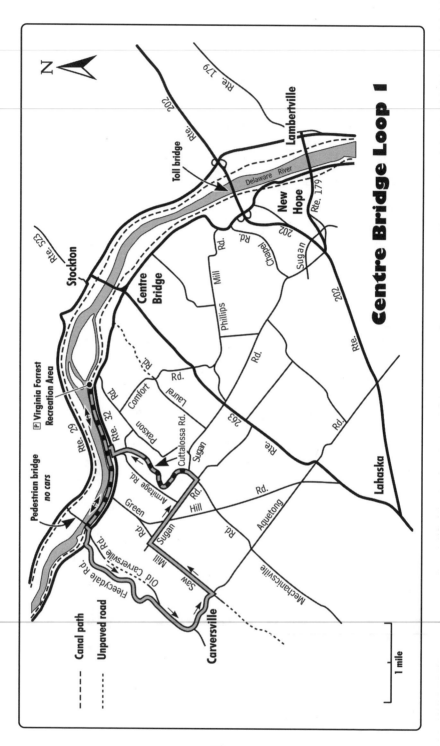

Centre Bridge Loop 1

Canal path
Unpaved road

1 mile

Centre Bridge Loop I

P **Virginia Forrest Recreation Area, Rte. 32, Solebury Twp.**

0.0	R	Towpath
2.0	L	Cross the canal using the bridge in Lumberville
	R	Rte. 32
2.2	L	Fleecydale Rd.
4.3	S	Aquetong Rd.
4.9	L	Saw Mill Rd.
5.9	R	Sugan Rd.
6.9	L	Sugan Rd.
7.2	L	Cuttalossa Rd.
8.5	R	Rte. 32
8.6	L	Bridge over canal at Delaware Quarries
8.6	R	Towpath
9.7	L	Return to Virginia Forrest Recreation Area

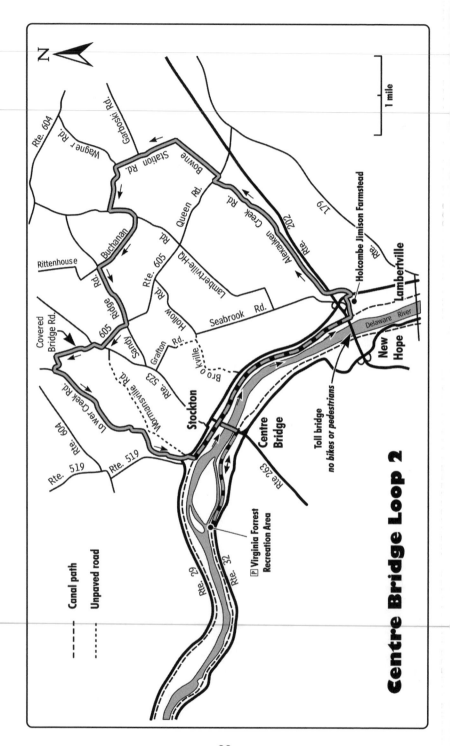

Centre Bridge Loop 2

88

Centre Bridge Loop 2

Mile	Dir	Location
P		Virginia Forrest Recreation Area, Rte. 32, Solebury Twp.
0.0	L	Towpath
1.2		Carry bike up stairs from towpath
	R	Bridge to N.J.
1.4	R	Delaware & Raritan Canal path
3.8	L	Driveway to Holcombe Jimison Farmstead
		JUST AFTER RTE. 202 TOLL BRIDGE
4.0	R	Rte. 29
4.1	L	Alexauken Creek Rd.
6.4	R	Queen Rd.
6.5	L	Bowne Station Rd.
8.7	L	Lambertville-Headquarters Rd.
9.1	R	Buchanan Rd.
10.0	L	Sandy Ridge Rd.
10.8	R	Rte. 605
11.2	R	Rte. 523
11.3	L	Covered Bridge Rd.
		! WATCH FOR TURNS AT BOTTOM OF HILL
12.1	L	Lower Creek Rd.
14.2	L	Rte. 519
14.3	S	Rte. 29
14.6	R	Entrance to Prallsville Mills
		FOLLOW DRIVE TO CANAL PATH BEHIND MILL BUILDINGS
14.7	L	Towpath
15.0	R	Bridge St.
	X	Bridge to Pa.
15.3	L	Carry bike down stairs to canal
	R	Towpath
16.7	R	Return to Virginia Forrest Recreation Area

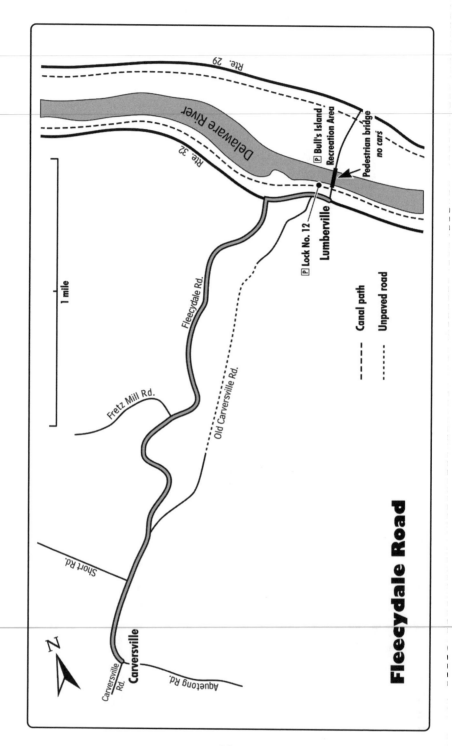

Fleecydale Road

Fleecydale Road

P **Bull's Island Recreation Area, Rte. 29, Stockton, N.J.**

0.0   Pedestrian bridge
RIDE NORTH ON RTE. 32

0.2 L Fleecydale Rd.

2.3   Arrive in Carversville
TURN AROUND AND GO BACK

4.4 R Rte. 32

4.6 L Return to
pedestrian bridge

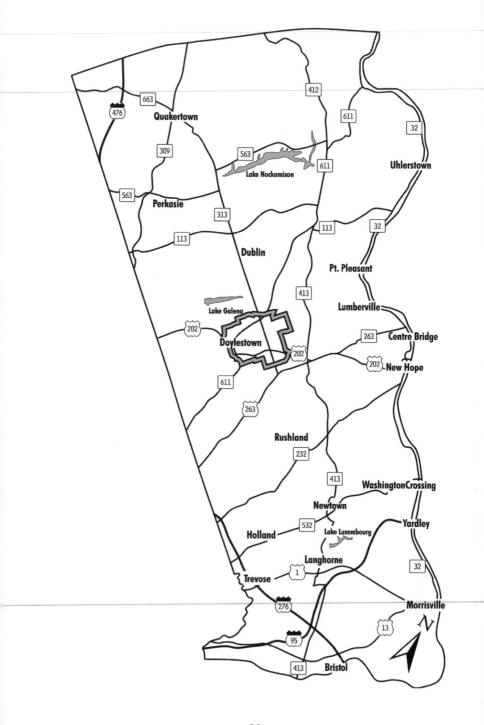

Doylestown

Distance: 15.2 miles

Start: Sauerman Park
Sauerman Road, Doylestown Township

Terrain: Mix of roads including town, residential, and
country, some with traffic; some hills

This ride goes all the way around Doylestown, the county seat. Sometimes it skirts the edges of the more heavily developed areas, and sometimes it follows roads through scenery that looks more rural than it really is.

No matter how it feels, this ride never leaves civilization very far behind. More than most routes in this book, it is suitable for experienced cyclists who are accustomed to riding in traffic. You'll encounter fewer cars if you ride early on a weekend morning, but it's a relative improvement.

The route begins at Sauerman Park and makes a counterclockwise circle around Doylestown. It crosses busy roads at several places where there are no traffic lights; be especially careful at those intersections.

There are lights where Saw Mill Road crosses Routes 611 and 313, but the busiest part of the ride comes just after these intersections. The roads here are still easily wide enough to accommodate bicycles, however. Farther on, you'll have the option of using part of the Doylestown bike & hike system to avoid traffic on Sandy Ridge Road.

The ride crosses Route 202 at the light on Iron Hill Road and goes through Delaware Valley College. Follow the campus road to the right past the large parking area, then bear left instead of going under the railroad tracks and exit onto New Britain Road.

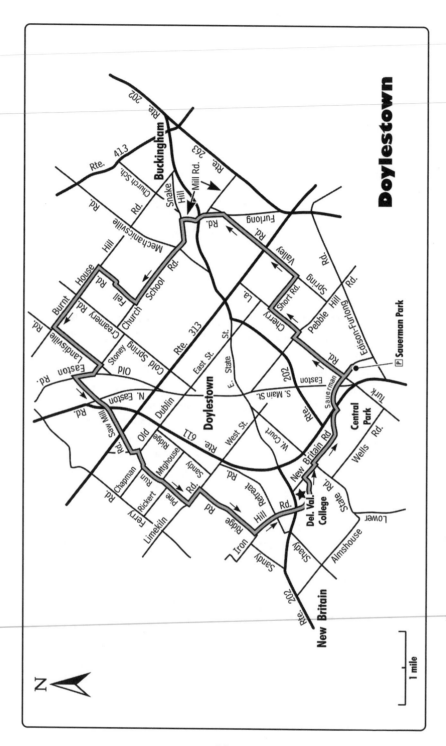

Doylestown

P Sauerman Park,
Sauerman Rd., Doylestown Twp.

Mile	Turn	Road
0.0	L	Sauerman Rd.
0.1	R	Turk Rd.
0.9	R	Pebble Hill Rd.
1.0	L	Cherry La.
1.6	R	Short Rd.
2.1	L	Spring Valley Rd.
2.7	X	Rte. 313
3.5	L	Furlong Rd.
3.7	L	Mill Rd.
3.8	X	Rte. 202
		! NO LIGHT; WATCH FOR TRAFFIC
4.1	L	Snake Hill Rd.
4.5	X	Mechanicsville Rd.
	S	Church School Rd.

Mile	Turn	Road
5.6	R	Fell Rd.
6.3	L	Burnt House Hill Rd.
6.8	X	Cold Spring Creamery Rd.
		! NO LIGHT; WATCH FOR TRAFFIC
7.3	L	Landisville Rd.
8.2	R	Stoney La.
8.4	R	Old Easton Rd.
8.6	L	Saw Mill Rd.
9.0	X	N. Easton Rd.
9.6	X	Rte. 313
	S	Pine Run Rd.
9.9	L	Old Dublin Pike
10.0	R	Pine Run Rd.
11.0	L	Limekiln Rd.
11.3	R	Sandy Ridge Rd.
		OPTIONAL: USE BIKE/HIKE PATH

Mile	Turn	Road
12.3	L	Iron Hill Rd.
12.9	X	Rte. 202/Butler Ave.
		RIDE THROUGH DELAWARE VALLEY COLLEGE
13.5	R	New Britain Rd.
13.8	X	Lower State Rd.
14.9	X	Easton Rd.
		! NO LIGHT; WATCH FOR TRAFFIC
15.2	R	Return to Sauerman Park

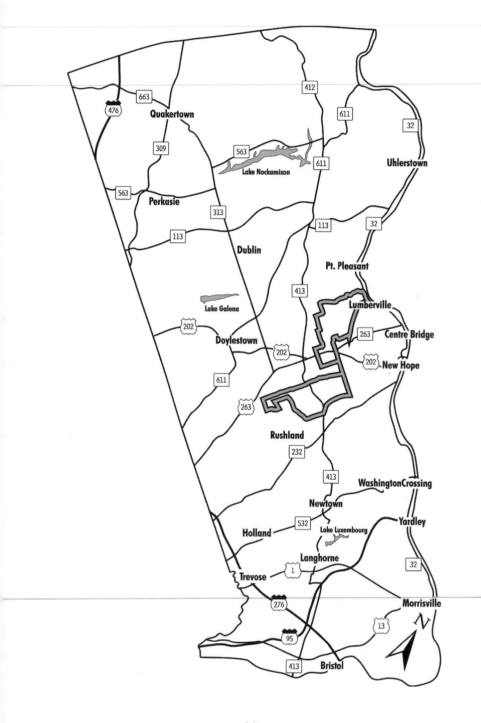

Holicong

Distance: 31.6 miles
Start: Holicong Park
Route 202, Buckingham Township
Terrain: A mix of roads; some hills
Variations: 15.5 and 24.5 miles, with a few short hills

This ride includes a variety of Bucks County landscapes, from views of the Delaware River to farmland along Neshaminy Creek and sweeping vistas to the south of Buckingham Mountain.

The route follows two of the most scenic roads in Bucks County: Fleecydale Road, which runs through the woods beside Paunnacussing Creek, and Ridge Road, which rolls through a swath of protected farmland.

The ride begins at Holicong Park on Route 202 in Buckingham Township. The park has a side entrance on Holicong Road, which doesn't carry much traffic except during the hours just before and after the school day, when it becomes a major thoroughfare to and from the Central Bucks school complex on the other side of Route 202.

The southern variation has a little more farmland, while the northern variation is more wooded, especially near Lumberville. The southern variation also carries more traffic in some areas, especially along Swamp Road, while the northern loop has fast-moving traffic on Route 32.

Peddler's Village is a tourist-oriented shopping destination that can be very busy, especially on weekends, but it makes an interesting rest stop. Lumberville also has a store where you can buy refreshments, and the pedestrian bridge across the Delaware there makes a pleasant detour.

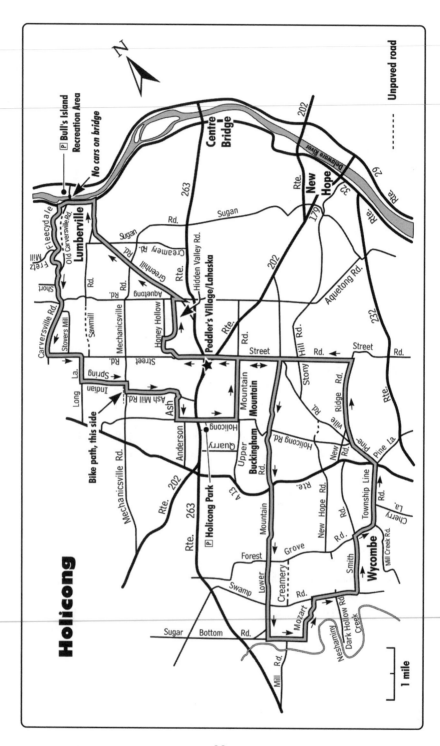

Holicong

N

P Bull's Island Recreation Area

No cars on bridge

Centre Bridge

New Hope

Delaware River

Rte. 32

Rte. 29

Rte. 179

202

263

Sugan Rd.

Sugan

Fleecydale Rd.

Old Carversville Rd.

Fretz Mill

Short

Lumberville

Creamery Rd.

Greenhill Rd.

Sugan Rd.

Hidden Valley Rd.

Aquetong

Aquetong Rd.

Rte. 232

Carversville Rd.

Stovers Mill

Sawmill Rd.

Mechanicsville

Honey Hollow Rd.

Peddler's Village/Lahaska

Rte.

Street

Street Rd.

Stony Hill Rd.

Street Rd.

Rte.

Bike path, this side

Long La.

Indian Spring La.

Ash Mill Rd.

Ash

Anderson

Quarry Rd.

Holicong

Upper Mountain Rd.

Buckingham Mountain

Holicong Rd.

ville Rd.

New Rd.

Ridge Rd.

Pine La.

Mechanicsville Rd.

Rte. 202

Rte. 263

P Holicong Park

Rte. 413

Mountain Rd.

New Hope Rd.

Rd.

Township Line Rd.

Cherry La.

Wycombe

Mill Creek Rd.

Forest Grove

Lower

Creamery Rd.

Smith Rd.

Swamp

Sugar Bottom Rd.

Mill Rd.

Mozart Rd.

Dark Hollow Rd.

Neshaminy Creek

1 mile

Unpaved road

98

Holicong

P		Holicong Park, Rte. 202, Buckingham Twp.
0.0	R	Holicong Rd.
		USE SIDE DRIVEWAY
0.6	L	Upper Mountain Rd.
1.8	R	Street Rd.
2.7	R	Lower Mountain Rd.
5.2	X	Rte. 413
!		NO LIGHT; WATCH FOR TRAFFIC
6.6	X	Forest Grove Rd.
7.5	X	Swamp Rd.
8.1	L	Sugar Bottom Rd.
8.9	L	Mozart Rd.
9.7	R	Swamp Rd.
10.6	L	Smith Rd.
11.7	R	Forest Grove Rd.
12.1	X	Wycombe bridge
	S	Township Line Rd.
13.4	X	Rte. 413
	S	Pineville Rd.
13.9	R	Ridge Rd.
15.6	L	Street Rd.
17.9	X	Rte. 202
18.5	X	Rte. 263
19.1	R	Honey Hollow Rd.
19.6	R	Hidden Valley Rd.
20.6	R	Aquetong Rd.
20.7	L	Greenhill Rd.
23.4	L	River Rd.
24.1	L	Fleecydale Rd.
26.2	R	Carversville Rd.
27.3	L	Street Rd.
28.0	R	Long La.
28.4	L	Indian Spring Rd.
29.3	R	Mechanicsville Rd.
		OPTIONAL: USE BIKE PATH
29.5	L	Ash Mill Rd.
30.6	R	Ash Rd.
31.0	L	Holicong Rd.
31.5	X	Rte. 202
31.6	R	Return to Holicong Park

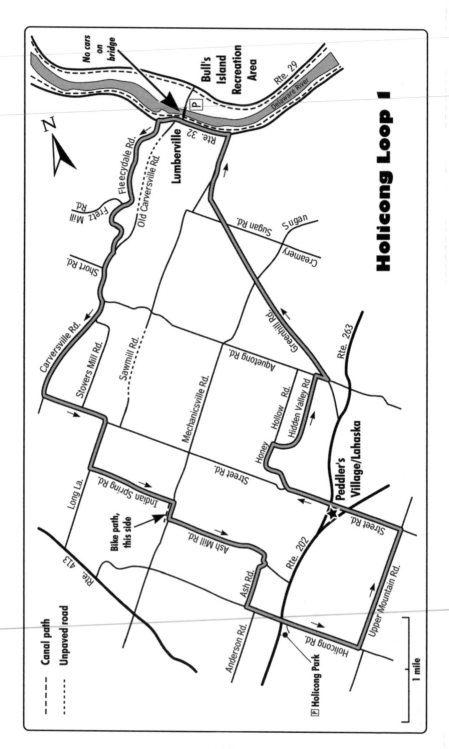

Holicong Loop 1

No cars on bridge

Bull's Island Recreation Area

Rte. 29

Delaware River

Rte. 32

Lumberville

Fleecydale Rd.

Old Carversville Rd.

Fretz Mill Rd.

Short Rd.

Carversville Rd.

Stovers Mill Rd.

Sawmill Rd.

Sugan Rd.

S ugan

Creamery

Greenhill Rd.

Aquetong Rd.

Mechanicsville Rd.

Honey Hollow Rd.

Hidden Valley Rd.

Rte. 263

Peddler's Village/Lahaska

Street Rd.

Street Rd.

Long La.

Indian Spring Rd.

Bike path, this side

Ash Mill Rd.

Ash Rd.

Rte. 202

Rte. 413

Anderson Rd.

Holicong Rd.

Upper Mountain Rd.

P Holicong Park

Canal path
Unpaved road

N

1 mile

Holicong Loop I

P Holicong Park,
Rte. 202, Buckingham Twp.

0.0 R Holicong Rd.
USE SIDE DRIVEWAY

0.6 L Upper Mountain Rd.

1.8 L Street Rd.

2.4 X Rte. 202

2.5 X Rte. 263

3.0 R Honey Hollow Rd.

3.5 R Hidden Valley Rd.

4.5 R Aquetong Rd.

4.6 L Greenhill Rd.

7.3 L Rte. 32

8.0 L Fleecydale Rd.

10.1 R Carversville Rd.

11.2 L Street Rd.

11.9 R Long La.

12.3 L Indian Spring Rd.

13.2 R Mechanicsville Rd.
OPTIONAL: USE BIKE PATH

13.4 L Ash Mill Rd.

14.5 R Ash Rd.

14.9 L Holicong Rd.

15.4 X Rte. 202

15.5 R Return to Holicong Park

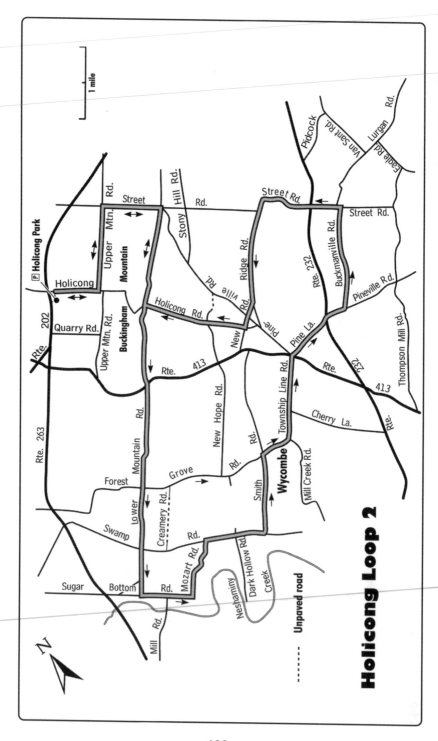

Holicong Loop 2

Holicong Loop 2

P Holicong Park,
Rte. 202, Buckingham Twp.

0.0	R	Holicong Rd. USE SIDE DRIVEWAY
0.6	L	Upper Mountain Rd.
1.8	R	Street Rd.
2.7	R	Lower Mountain Rd.
5.2	X	Rte. 413 **!** NO LIGHT; WATCH FOR TRAFFIC
6.6	X	Forest Grove Rd.
7.5	X	Swamp Rd.
8.1	L	Sugar Bottom Rd.
8.9	L	Mozart Rd.
9.7	R	Swamp Rd.
10.6	L	Smith Rd.
11.7	R	Forest Grove Rd.
12.1	X	Wycombe bridge
13.3	S X	Township Line Rd. Rte. 413 WALK IN FRONT OF PINEVILLE TAVERN TO PINE LA.
13.4	L	Pine La.
14.1	X S	Rte. 232 Pineville Rd.
14.5	L	Buckmanville Rd.
15.9	L	Street Rd.
16.3	X	Rte. 232
17.2	S	Ridge Rd.
18.5	BR	New Rd.
18.9	R	Holicong Rd.
20.4	R	Lower Mountain Rd.
21.8	L	Street Rd.
22.6	L	Upper Mountain Rd.
23.8	R	Holicong Rd.
24.5	L	Return to Holicong Park

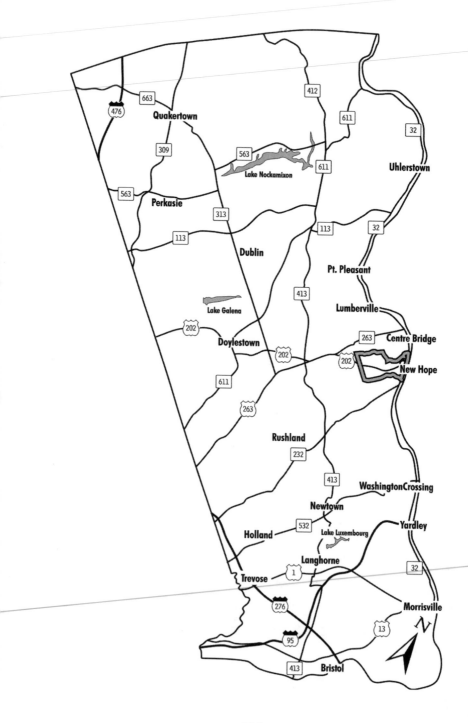

New Hope

Distance: 10.1 miles

Start: New Hope Information Center
South Main and Mechanic Streets, New Hope

Terrain: Mix of roads, some with traffic; a few small hills

A Bucks County bicycling book without a New Hope ride would seem incomplete, since that bustling river town is the area's unofficial tourism capital. Parking in New Hope can be a problem, though, and one of the primary requirements for the rides in this book is the availability of free parking near the start of the route.

New Hope's on-street parking is metered, and the town's hawk-eyed enforcers rarely miss a chance to write a ticket, which could mean a hefty fine if your ride takes longer than planned. At peak tourist times, it can be hard to find a space.

One way to get around this is to park outside of New Hope and ride your bike into town. Both the Virginia Forrest Recreation Center and Bowman's Hill Wildlife Preserve have free parking near the Delaware Canal towpath a few miles from New Hope. See pages 3, 82, and 108 for information about these facilities. Another possibility is to ride before 10 A.M., when the meters go into effect.

The route begins at the New Hope Information Center at S. Main and Mechanic Streets, where you can pick up information about shops and galleries and peruse the menus of local restaurants when your ride is done. If you take the towpath all the way back to Mechanic Street, you'll have to carry your bike up some steps to the street, but you will pass other places where you can leave the towpath at street level.

New Hope

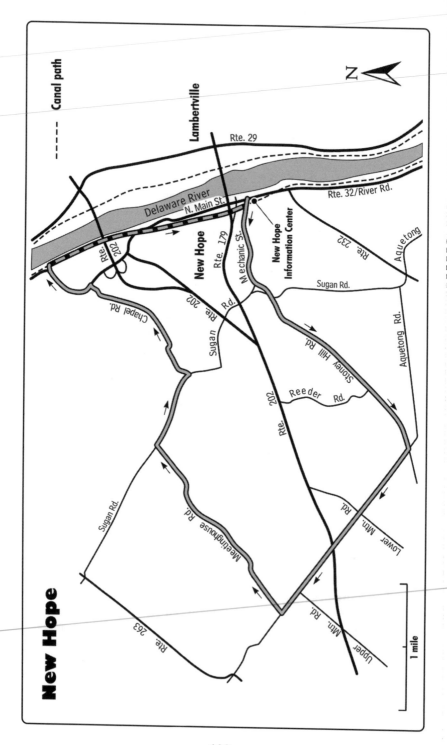

New Hope

**New Hope Information Center,
S. Main & Mechanic Sts.,
New Hope**

0.0 L Mechanic St.

0.7 L Stoney Hill Rd.

0.8 S Stoney Hill Rd.

2.6 R Aquetong Rd.

3.6 X Rte. 202

4.3 R Meetinghouse Rd.

6.1 R Sugan Rd.

6.7 L Chapel Rd.

7.9 L Rte. 32

8.3 R small road between
buildings to bridge over
canal

8.4 R towpath

9.9 X Bridge St.

10.0 L Mechanic St.
CARRY BIKE UP STEPS TO STREET

10.1 R Return to New Hope
Information Center

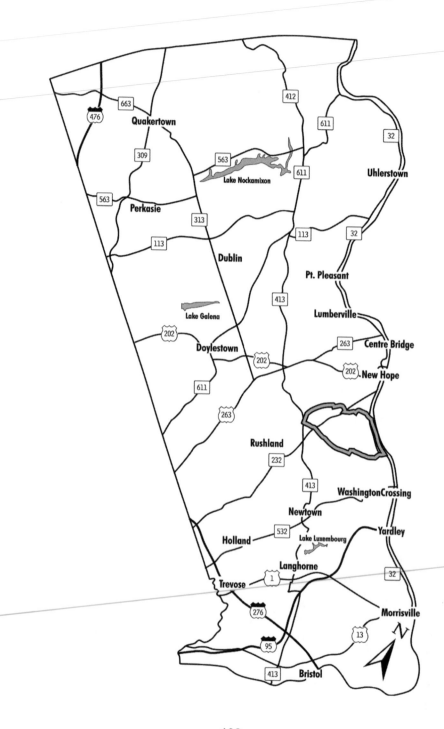

Bowman's Hill

Distance:	13.8 miles
Start:	Bowman's Hill Wildflower Preserve Route 32, Solebury Township
Terrain:	Mix of roads, some with traffic; rolling
Variations:	11.7 and 11.0 miles on rolling roads; some traffic

Bowman's Hill is best known for its wildflower preserve showcasing nearly a thousand species of plants native to Pennsylvania. Thanks to its location on Route 32 along the Delaware Canal, it's also a good place to start a bike ride.

For cycling purposes, it's best to park in the eastern part of the park, near the Delaware Canal. (See page 3 for more information on cycling the canal.) The exit from this area is directly across Route 32 from Aquetong Road, which leads inland toward some scenic areas south of New Hope. Ridge Road, for example, runs through an unspoiled area of protected farmland. Van Sant Road passes through the Van Sant Covered Bridge, which was built in 1875 and is the last of the old covered bridges left in this part of the county.

Some of these roads carry more traffic than the rest. Be especially careful on the section of Route 32 between the towpath and Stony Brook Road, as well as the short piece of Route 232 between the two segments of Pidcock Creek Road.

If you have time to extend your visit with some non-cycling activities, stop at the visitor center at the Wildflower Preserve for a copy of the map detailing the preserve's well-maintained trail system. Nearby Bowman's Tower, located off Lurgan Road, offers a panoramic view of surrounding countryside for a small fee. You'll have to drive there, however, because official policy is that no bicycles are allowed up the hill to the tower.

Bowman's Hill

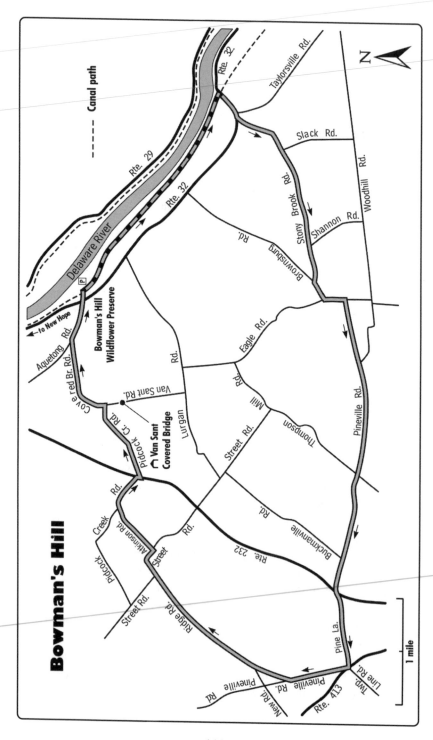

Canal path

Rte. 29

Delaware River

to New Hope

Rte. 32

Rte. 32

Rte. 32

Taylorsville Rd.

Slack Rd.

Stony Brook Rd.

Shannon Rd.

Woodhill Rd.

Brownsburg Rd.

Eagle Rd.

Pineville Rd.

Aquetong Rd.

Covered Br. Rd.

Bowman's Hill Wildflower Preserve

Van Sant Rd.

Van Sant Covered Bridge

Pidcock Cr. Rd.

Lurgan Rd.

Mill Rd.

Thompson Rd.

Street Rd.

Creek Rd.

Pidcock Creek Rd.

Atkinson Rd.

Street Rd.

Street Rd.

Rte. 232

Buckmanville Rd.

Ridge Rd.

New Rd.

Pineville Rd.

Pineville Rd.

Rte. 413

Pine La.

Twp. Line Rd.

1 mile

Bowman's Hill

P		Bowman's Hill, Rte. 32, Solebury Twp.
0.0	L	Ride south on towpath
2.5	S	Walk bike up to road at bridge
	R	Rte. 32
2.6	L	Stony Brook Rd.
4.4	S	Stony Brook Rd.
4.6	L	Eagle Rd.
4.8	R	Pineville Rd.
7.6	X	Rte. 232
	S	Pine La.
8.4	R	Rte. 413
		WALK IN FRONT OF PINEVILLE TAVERN TO PINEVILLE RD.
8.5	R	Pineville Rd.
9.0	R	Ridge Rd.
10.7	S	Street Rd.
11.0	L	Atkinson Rd.
11.5	S	Pidcock Creek Rd.
11.8	R	Rte. 232
11.8	L	Pidcock Creek Rd.
12.7	L	Covered Bridge Rd.
13.5	R	Aquetong Rd.
13.8	X	Rte. 32
	S	Return to Bowman's Hill parking area

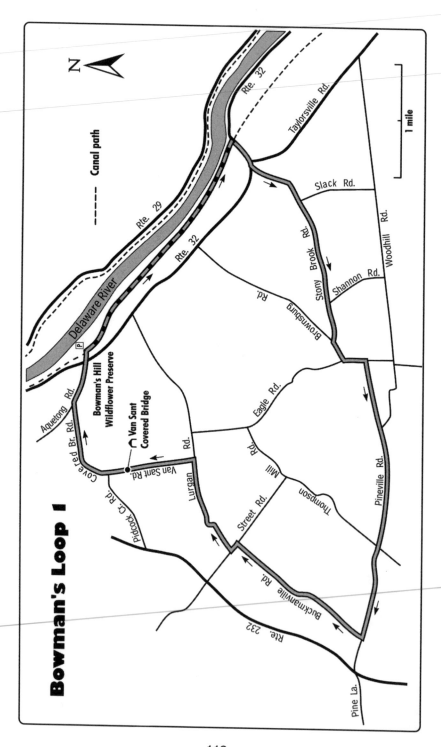

Bowman's Loop 1

N

Canal path
Rte. 29

Delaware River

Rte. 32

Rte. 32

Taylorsville Rd.

1 mile

P

Bowman's Hill
Wildflower Preserve

Van Sant
Covered Bridge

Aquetong Rd.

Covered Br. Rd.

Pidcock Cr. Rd.

Van Sant Rd.

Lurgan Rd.

Slack Rd.

Stony Brook Rd.

Shannon Rd.

Woodhill Rd.

Brownsburg Rd.

Eagle Rd.

Mill Rd.

Thompson

Street Rd.

Pineville Rd.

Buckmanville Rd.

Rte. 232

Pine La.

Bowman's Loop I

P		**Bowman's Hill,**
		Rte. 32, Solebury Twp.
0.0	L	Ride south on towpath
2.3	S	Walk bike up to road at bridge
	R	Rte. 32
2.6	L	Stony Brook Rd.
4.6	L	Eagle Rd.
4.8	R	Pineville Rd.
7.3	R	Buckmanville Rd.
8.7	L	Street Rd.
8.8	R	Lurgan Rd.
9.7	L	Van Sant Rd.
		BECOMES COVERED BRIDGE RD.
11.3	R	Aquetong Rd.
11.7	X	Rte. 32
	S	Return to Bowman's Hill parking area

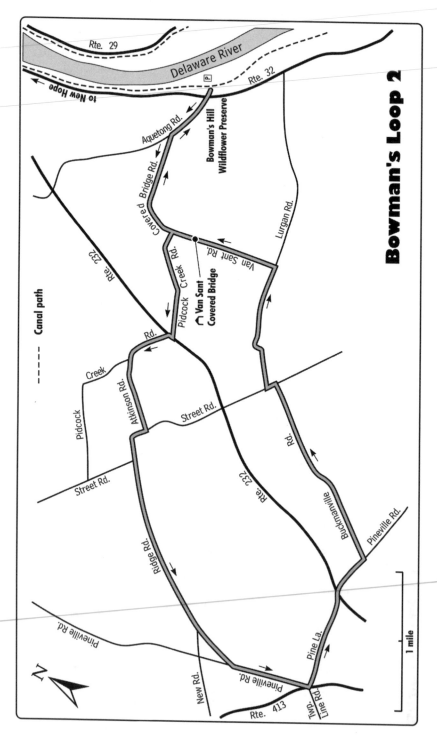

Bowman's Loop 2

Canal path

1 mile

Bowman's Loop 2

P Bowman's Hill,
Rte. 32, Solebury Twp.

0.0	X	Rte. 32
	S	Aquetong Rd.
0.3	L	Covered Bridge Rd.
1.1	R	Pidcock Creek Rd.
2.0	R	Rte. 232
2.0	L	Pidcock Creek Rd.
2.4	S	Atkinson Rd.
2.9	R	Street Rd.
3.1	S	Ridge Rd.
4.9	L	Pineville Rd.
5.4	L	Rte. 413
		WALK BIKE IN FRONT OF PINEVILLE TAVERN TO PINE LA.
5.5	L	Pine La.
6.2	X	Rte. 232
6.5	S	Pineville Rd.
	L	Buckmanville Rd.
7.9	L	Street Rd.
8.0	R	Lurgan Rd.
8.9	L	Van Sant Rd.
		BECOMES COVERED BRIDGE RD.
10.5	R	Aquetong Rd.
10.9	X	Rte. 32
	S	Return to Bowman's Hill parking area

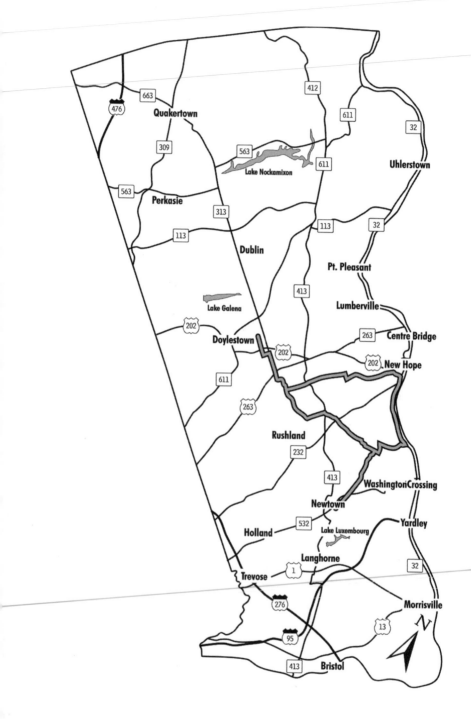

New Hope-Newtown-Doylestown

Distance: New Hope to Newtown, 11.7
Newtown to Doylestown, 15.9
Doylestown to New Hope, 12.0

Terrain: Mix of roads, some heavily traveled; hilly

Although these three routes include some nice scenery, they are provided here primarily for utilitarian reasons. They allow cyclists to travel between New Hope, Newtown, and Doylestown, three of the largest towns in Bucks County, while avoiding major roads like Routes 202 and 413.

The towns are connected in pairs, rather than in a continuous loop, so it isn't necessary to ride the entire circuit. All three routes can be followed in either direction.

There are some hills on each of the routes, and some of the roads may carry a fair amount of automobile traffic, especially late weekday afternoons.

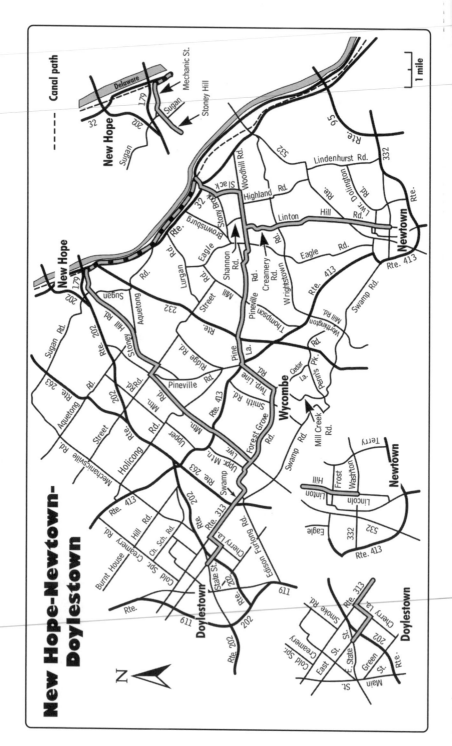

New Hope-Newtown-Doylestown

------ Canal path

1 mile

New Hope to Newtown

S. Main. & Mechanic Sts., New Hope

0.0		Ride south on S. Main St.
0.2	L	When canal goes under S. Main St. and towpath appears to end, cross S. Main and follow gravel drive past houses and through Odette's parking lot
0.3	L, R	Cross canal on bridge next to Odette's and resume towpath
4.4	S	Walk bike up to road at bridge
	R	Rte. 32
4.8	L	Stony Brook Rd.
5.3	L	Slack Rd.
6.0	R	Woodhill Rd.
7.1	L	Creamery Rd.
8.1	X	Wrightstown Rd.
	S	Linton Hill Rd.
11.2	X	Frost La.
	S	N. Lincoln Ave.
11.7		Washington Ave., Newtown

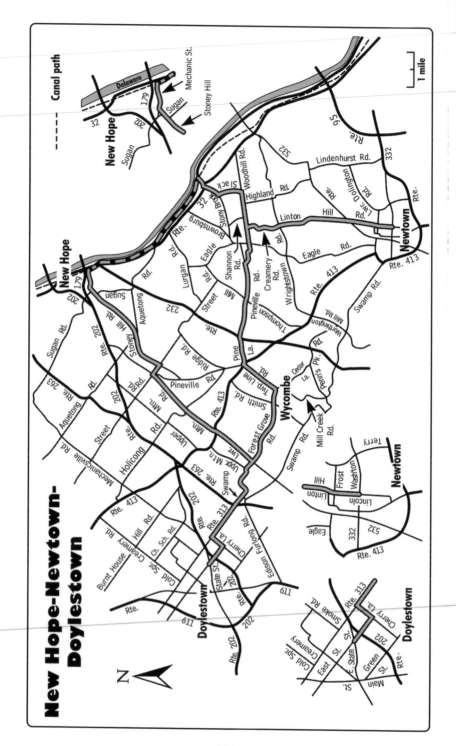

New Hope-Newtown-Doylestown

Newtown to Doylestown

Washington & Lincoln Aves., Newtown

0.0		Ride north on N. Lincoln Ave.
0.4	X	Frost La.
	S	Linton Hill Rd.
3.5	X	Wrightstown Rd.
	S	Creamery Rd.
4.5	L	Woodhill Rd.
5.0	X	Eagle Rd.
	S	Woodhill Rd.
5.6	L	Pineville Rd.
7.8	X	Rte. 232
	S	Pine La.
8.6	R	Rte. 413

WALK IN FRONT OF PINEVILLE TAVERN TO LIGHT

8.6	L	Township Line Rd.
9.9	X	Wycombe bridge
	S	Forest Grove Rd.
13.3	S	Swamp Rd.
		FOREST GROVE RD. GOES LEFT
13.6	X	Rte. 263
	S	Rte. 313
14.8	L	Cherry La.
15.2	R	East St.
15.9		E. State St.

New Hope-Newtown-Doylestown

Doylestown to New Hope

**East St. & E. State St.,
Doylestown**

0.0		Ride southeast on East St.
0.7	L	Cherry La.
1.1	R	Rte. 313
2.2	X	Rte. 263
2.6	L	Forest Grove Rd.
3.8	L	Lower Mtn. Rd.
5.2	X	Rte. 413
7.8	R	Street Rd.
8.1	L	Stoney Hill Rd.
11.1	BR	W. Mechanic St.
12.0		S. Main St.

Resources

Freewheeling Press
PO Box 540
Lahaska PA 18931
www.freewheelingpress.com

Our web site has more information about cycling in Bucks County, links to related sites, and the latest updates to these rides.

Bike Clubs

Central Bucks Bicycle Club
PO Box 1648
Doylestown PA 18901
www.cbbikeclub.org

Suburban Cyclists Unlimited
Box 401
Horsham PA 19044
www.suburbancyclists.org

Tourism

Bucks County Conference & Visitors Bureau
3207 Street Road
Bensalem PA 19020
(215) 639-0300 (800) 836-BUCKS
www.buckscountycvb.org

New Hope Borough Information Center
South Main and Mechanic Streets
New Hope PA 18938
(215) 862-5880

Rides by distance

Ride	Miles	Terrain	Page
Fleecydale Road	4.6	Gently rolling country road	90
Hilltown Loop 2	6.6	Rolling country roads	80
Ringing Rocks variation	8.2	Rolling country roads	54
Lake Loop 1	9.5	Hilly country roads	68
Centre Bridge Loop 1	9.7	Mix of roads, mostly rolling with some hills; 1 mile on unpaved road; 3.1 miles on towpath	86
New Hope	10.1	Mix of roads, some with traffic; a few small hills	104
Lake Loop 2	10.1	Hilly country roads	70
Haycock Loop 1	10.2	Rolling country roads; wide shoulder on Rte. 563	46
Bowman's Loop 2	10.9	Mix of roads, some with traffic; rolling	114
Dublin	11.5	Rolling country roads	72

Ride	Miles	Terrain	Page
New Hope-Newtown	11.7	Mix of roads, some heavily traveled; hilly	116
Bowman's Loop I	11.7	Mix of roads, some with traffic; rolling	112
Ottsville Loop I	11.8	Country roads; hilly, with a very steep downhill approaching the covered bridge; 0.4 miles unpaved	60
Spinnerstown	12.0	Country roads; some hills	28
Doylestown-New Hope	12.0	Mix of roads, some heavily traveled; hilly	116
Trumbauersville	13.4	Country roads; some hills	32
Haycock Loop 2	13.5	Rolling country roads; wide shoulder on Rte. 563	48
Ottsville Loop 2	13.5	Hilly country roads	62
Bowman's Hill	13.8	Mix of roads, some with traffic; rolling	108
Hilltown Loop I	14.0	Hilly country roads	78
Doylestown	15.2	Mix of roads including town, residential, and country, some with traffic; some hills	92
Holicong Loop I	15.5	A mix of roads with some hills	100

Ride	Miles	Terrain	Page
Newtown-Doylestown	15.9	Mix of roads, some heavily traveled; hilly	116
Unami variation	16.4	Country roads; hilly; 0.8 miles unpaved	40
Centre Bridge Loop 2	16.7	Mix of roads with some hills; 5.3 miles on towpath	88
Hilltown	18.0	Country roads with some hills	74
Haycock Mountain	19.6	Rolling country roads; wide shoulder on Rte. 563	42
Lake to Lake	19.6	Country roads; hilly, especially near lakes	64
Ottsville	20.0	Country roads; hilly, with a very steep downhill approaching the covered bridge; 0.4 miles unpaved	56
Unami Creek	23.8	Country roads; hilly; 0.8 miles unpaved	36
Ringing Rocks	24.1	Rolling country roads with a few hills; 1 mile unpaved	50
Holicong Loop 2	24.5	A mix of roads with some hills	102
Centre Bridge	26.1	Mix of roads with some hills; 1 mile on unpaved road; 8.2 miles on towpath	82
Holicong	31.6	A mix of roads; some hills	96

Buy a book

Use this form to order books from Freewheeling Press, or look for more information about ordering online at www.freewheelingpress.com.

Name:

Address:

Telephone:

No.	Title	Price	Total
	Back Roads Bicycling in Bucks County, Pa. Features more than 40 rides on bike paths and scenic roads, with detailed maps and descriptions in a bike-friendly format.	$14.95	
	Mountain Biking in New Jersey More than 40 off-road rides in the Garden State, each accompanied by descriptive text and a detailed map with everything you need to know to enjoy each ride.	$14.95	
	Walking Bucks County, Pa. A guide to walks on country roads, paved paths, and woodland trails in this scenic area, with maps.	$12.95	
	Freewheeling Press Bike Journal Personal bike touring journal opens flat for easy writing, with space to record directions, distance, difficulty, and other details of your rides.	$12.95	
	The Back Roads Bike Book Maps and directions for a dozen short scenic rides in and around Lambertville, N.J., and New Hope, Pa., with info on things to see and do, places to stay.	$12.95	

Send to:

Freewheeling Press
PO Box 540
Lahaska PA 18931

Shipping ($2 per book)	
Subtotal	
Pa. residents add 6% tax	
Grand total	

Make check payable to Freewheeling Press